A Man of Peace Goes to War

a memoir

Isaac "Harold" Storey

with James Arthur Douglas and Dekie Hicks

© 2020
Published in the United States by Nurturing Faith Inc., Macon GA,
www.nurturingfaith.net.

Nurturing Faith is the book publishing arm of Good Faith Media (goodfaithmedia.org).

Library of Congress Cataloging-in-Publication Data is available.

ISBN: 978-1-63528-122-4

To the countless lives of friends, brothers, and heroes defending freedom itself against pure evil. To those who have walked before me and those who follow behind, here is our story.

Isaac "Harold" Storey

Contents

Preface

James Arthur Douglas

Friends and family, old and young have lined the edges of the yard with hundreds of small American flags placed in the ground; their colors brightly reflected under a blue, cloudless sky. A young man at heart holds one small American flag between his aged hands, which, seventy-five years ago, defended the very freedom it represents. Although the man with the flag will never admit it, he is a hero. He has saved hundreds of lives, led young American soldiers into the toughest battles in human history, and made incredible sacrifices for his country and mankind. I am also lucky to call him my friend, especially today, the afternoon of his ninety-eighth birthday.

I have known Mr. Storey my entire life. Raised in Rome, Georgia, I got to know him as a beloved member of our community and church. From my earliest memories, I remember being greeted by Mr. Storey with the biggest smile and kindest words. Moving on to high school and then to college, this never changed. To this day, Mr. Storey is always one of the first faces I see when I return home, and he never fails to enthusiastically exclaim, "Hey there, Sport!" every time I walk in his front door.

One afternoon, I received a phone call from Mr. Storey asking me to "get on over" to his house. He showed me down to his basement where he had organized his old uniform, helmet, and canteen, along with hundreds of handwritten notes, newspaper clippings, magazine articles, books, and pictures that all described and depicted different stories and tales of his service in World War II. Over the next few hours, he took the time to describe the significance and story that went along with each piece. Mr. Storey then sat me down and said, "Hey, Sport. Thank you for coming over. For over seventy years, hundreds of people, like you, have come over to listen to my stories. I wanted to ask if you would help me to write them all down in a book that I can give away to many more people who don't know my whole story.

It took me a few moments to process the question that had just been asked. I was honored to help in any way that I could, but there was one problem. As we walked back upstairs, I said, "Mr. Storey, I think that this is a fantastic idea, but I do not think that I am qualified. First of all, I don't know much about World War II. Secondly, I think the longest paper I have ever written was about junior year of college... and I think that one was only about eight pages." He slowly turned around and handed me a frame that displayed a Purple Heart and a Silver Star. He looked back up at me, put one hand on my shoulder and simply said, "Sport, don't worry about all that. If there is one thing that I do know, I already like the way you will help share my story.

And so, we started from the very beginning and compiled each story one by one. I would usually take these stories back home to write, but every so often, I would mix up a few stories and have to go ask for clarification. There was one day that I drove up to Mr. Storey's house and all of their cars were gone. I have him a quick call and said "Mr. Storey, are you home? I need to ask you a few quick questions." He said, "No, I am not home now, I am running errands all over town and currently trying on new clothes at the mall. I should be back later this afternoon." This was shortly after his ninety-seventh birthday. I just laughed at the fact that I usually do not even have enough energy to go to the mall.

A Man of Peace Goes to War is just that: a compilation of the very stories Mr. Storey has carried with him for over seventy-five years, shared with thousands of people through writing and oral interviews, and repeated again to me. In order to help "fill in the gaps" between his stories, I have included sections of a piece titled *The History of Company C, 10th Infantry U.S. Inf. Fifth Division, in the Battle of Europe*. Lieutenant Robert Dunn worked closely with Mr. Storey and several other members of the company shortly after the war to compile and write *The History of Company C*. This piece tells the complete history of Mr. Storey's company during the war and gives a thorough overview of the locations and dates that correspond with Mr. Storey's retellings. *The History of Company C* was never published, and only used as a reference between the veterans of Company C after the war.

It took me a while to wrap my head around the fact that I started working on this project at twenty-one years old, the same age as Mr.

Storey when he left for Europe. With great help from author and editor Dekie Hicks, as well as members from Mr. Storey's family, I am honored to help tell his story.

If there is one thing I have learned, friendship knows no age. And so, this is the story of my friend, a hero.

James Arthur Douglas

Foreword

Bill Henderson

Nowhere can we learn more of the experience of World War II than through the eyes and ears of a soldier. These pages reveal an inside view of the challenges facing a soldier, an everyday young man from the hills of North Georgia. Harold Storey was a student at the University of Georgia when the news came about the war. He tells his story, sometimes with bare and sordid detail, as if writing to his home folks. After reading this, we can say, as did General Sherman, "War is hell!"

Inside these pages you will read about the irony of this soldier landing in the same town where his father of an earlier generation landed on European soil for "the war to end all wars," World War I.

You will read about frightening assignments, impossible odds, intensely personal loyalties along with the lands of France, Germany, Belgium, and Luxembourg and the hospitals of England when the almost inevitable yet unbelievable occurred for Harold Storey, "Wounded in action!"

The most important things to learn in these first-person accounts are the processes and decisions that made this war the decisive event in history that won our freedom. Yes, there are decisions in the boardroom, the war room, but there are also the unusually personal and seemingly insignificant daily decisions that one Georgia boy had to make without any more preparation than a good heart, a trusty sense of love and duty, and an ability to see what had to be done and the courage to do it, no matter the cost personally or nationally.

This is the story of a soldier. This is the story of a courageous man. This is the story of all of those who when faced with a cruel and outrageous event in our world, even continents apart, will stand up tall and say, "Send me!" Read these details and think about the many individuals all over this nation—the families, the factories and farms, the schools and neighborhoods—who produced and nurtured their hearts, their minds, and their will. Think of the many Americans who willingly went then, and those who would go now, to defend our precious freedom. Then imagine yourself along with them.

W. G. Henderson Jr., 1LT, U.S. Army Reserves (son-in-law)

Introduction

Harold Storey

As I recall the experiences I have had over the ninety-eight years of my life, I realize that just as my ancestors who, as blacksmiths, shaped raw metal to produce the tools and equipment needed by the farmers and others in their community, so have I tried to use my talents and skills to meet the challenges of life in a way that might bring harmony and peace to my family and everyone I meet.

As in everybody's life, there have been difficult times in mine, but times of peace and harmony are worth fighting for. I am thankful to have known many caring, committed people and join them in trying to make the right things happen.

I have always felt "protected," as though I have a guardian angel on my shoulder who watches out for me. I have spent my whole life trying to help others not only in my community of Rome, Georgia, but as an infantryman in Europe in WWII and as one of the heirs to my father's lumber business. I prefer to work with people who have a clear vision and a goal and then help them to succeed. I do not aim for leadership, although somehow it seems as though I always end up in a leadership role.

The guys I was with in combat were amazing human beings. The people they are and were provide me with an inspiration to tell their story as well as mine and is one of the many reasons that drive me to write this book. These words are dedicated to them—to the countless lives of friends, brothers, and heroes defending freedom itself against pure evil. Seventy-five years later, they live on with me and in the stories of brotherhood, fellowship, and combat that you will soon read.

This book is also dedicated to those who have entered my life in the last seventy-five years. Snippets of my time overseas are compiled in many books, school projects, oral interviews, and hearts of those who take time to listen.

To those who have walked before me and those who follow behind, here is our story.

Isaac "Harold" Storey

The Early Years

I was born in Chattooga County, Georgia, on September 21, 1922, and I have lived all my life on one side or the other of the Floyd/Chattooga County line. I am a "Georgia boy" through and through, just like my parents who lived their entire lives in that neck of the woods. Shortly after I was born, my parents moved back to Floyd County from Chattooga County, where they bought the old sawmill built by my great-grandfather Pinkney Means.

My only sibling, Bernard, was born in June 1924. Bernard inherited my father's engineering mind. One of my first memories of my younger brother is me standing on the edge of my brother's crib begging him not to cry. It sounds kind of silly, but I've been trying to keep people from crying nearly all my life.

Another story that has been told to me is about my faithful companion Old Jack, a pointer bird dog. Jack was around me almost all the time. On one particular day, while my parents were picking cotton, chopping, and hoeing, we were sitting on top of an old quilt on the edge of a cotton field. Jack started barking frantically. A large snake had crawled up to the edge of the quilt. My father, Sike, came running up and killed the snake with a hoe. Jack then grabbed the snake with his mouth and slung it back and forth to punish it further. Even though I was told that he was first jealous of me when I was born, Jack was my constant companion and protector. I remember him being at my side all the time until his death one night due to a sudden illness.

Our school went from first grade to eleventh grade and was very small. At that time there was no twelfth grade and only fifteen kids in each grade. I was a protector, and I was always looking out for my younger brother. I remember one kid in particular who was bigger than all the other kids. My brother used to tell this story that we were walking up the hill from the basketball court to the school when the big kid said something to provoke and anger my younger brother. My younger brother has always said that I then picked up this kid and stood him on his head in a hole that had been dug to plant a tree. He said I was the hero for the rest of the afternoon. Looking back on this story as an adult, I hope I did not hurt that kid that day. Then again, things are a bit more exaggerated when you are so young!

I worked at the sawmill every day that I wasn't in school or doing something else. Storey's Mill was actually several mills: a steam-powered sawmill, a steam-powered cotton gin, and a gristmill powered by water. When the farmers would bring their wagons loaded with cotton to the cotton gin, my job was to mark each mule-drawn wagon's place in line with a piece of chalk so nobody could cut ahead of anyone else. Those farmers could get mighty upset if someone tried to get ahead of them in line.

We had a lot of cotton then. Roosevelt put programs into place that helped farmers during the hard times. Before and during the depression, farmers were getting five cents a pound for ginned cotton (the finished bale). This was less than it cost to grow. So based on this and a number of other factors, the government allotted farmers a certain number of acres they could plant. Anything over that number would have to be plowed under. This caused the price of cotton to rise to twelve cents a pound. We had scrip books, and when a farmer brought in his cotton, we'd cut out a certain amount of scrip, which would represent the amount of cotton that we ginned. This was the farmer's proof that he grew the right amount.

One of my cousins, Elton Perry, who attended the University of Georgia with me, would take off from school during the cotton season and help our family in the cotton gin. He received a master's degree and worked in agriculture extension, and his sister, Myrtle, received a master's degree in library science from UGA. They had me to dinner many times and helped me to overcome my homesickness during my first quarter at the University of Georgia.

My father grew up with the nickname "Sike" (pronounced "saɪk-ī"). My father was educated at the Donald Frasier Military Academy in Decatur, Georgia. One of his teachers, Sam Jones, who helped found the academy, took Sike with him there when he moved from the small one-room schoolhouse that Sike attended. Sike was a talented football player and turned down a football scholarship at Georgia Tech to enter the Army. When he went to Europe to fight in WWI, he landed in Greenock, Scotland, where I would land twenty-seven years later. My father drove a Model-T ambulance, helping with the evacuation of injured soldiers in France in the Meuse-Argonne area. This area was where the trench warfare was horrible; both sides used mustard gas. Part of this area is Verdun, where my division was forced to stop when the Red Ball Express exceeded its capacity to resupply the infantry. I claim to have slept in a few of his foxholes.

In 1920, when my father returned from the war, he married Stella Perry, who came from the Zachariah and Georgia Perry family, who lived just a couple of miles away from the Storey family. She had seven brothers and three sisters, including twin brothers who were two years older. One older brother, Clyde, was a blacksmith, and another brother, Grady, was a store merchant. Her father died in 1919, leaving her mother with seven children at home. Stella was one of the youngest, and, as you can imagine, she helped every one of her siblings during troubled times and at the end of their lives. My parents were very peaceful and caring people. My mother was soft-spoken.

Both of my parents worked in the family business. My mother was cofounder, the bookkeeper, and kept the office organized. Although he wasn't educated as an engineer, my father had a sixth sense about engineering problems that allowed him to tend to many mechanical issues that arose. There were enough problems around the mill to keep him busy all the time.

My dad was Presbyterian. My family helped support two different churches, the old Bethel Presbyterian Church in Chattooga county and Unity Baptist, where we attended Sunday school growing up. Church socials were a big entertainment in those days, and I loved attending "dinner on the grounds." To this day I love fried chicken, especially drumsticks, pimiento cheese sandwiches, and caramel cake.

I never knew my grandfather, Pickney Moses, who was a black-smith. He died in 1901 from appendicitis. My grandmother was Ella Selman. She lived about a mile away from us with her daughter, my Aunt Lona Mae, whom we called "Lady." These two women spoiled me. I always wanted to be a part of whatever they were doing, including chores around the house such as hanging out the linen wash, gathering firewood and fat lighter. Our big kitchen table was a gathering place for the family and for visitors. Lady would take me to relatives' houses in the Texas Valley, to church at Old Armuchee, or to visit other neighbors.

They originally lived up at the old Storey's Mill. It was pretty isolated up there, and they moved in with us when I was about six years old. It was not long after they moved in with us that my dad moved the grist mill and sawmill close to Crystal Spring, where my dad had bought an interest in an old cotton gin.

My mom and grandmother were quite the gardeners. There were flowers and sweet peas on a fence that ran the full length of the garden along the approach to the house. My grandmother had a thing about roses. We didn't have all the sophisticated rows and hybrid plants that we have now, and back then people would exchange cuttings for in-season vegetables. We had a nice garden plot. I cleared out a little place next to the rose garden and planted a garden of my own. The only thing I remember is having some irises that did well.

My grandmother played the piano and sang terribly. The mother of one of the kids at school played the piano, and she came on certain days to give piano lessons. I signed up to take lessons and earned the nickname "Sissy," but I didn't mind it. After she stopped giving lessons, we got a new English teacher, Valerie Lyden, from South Carolina, who also gave music lessons during lunch and after school. I remember her as a kind person who wanted us to learn and was popular with all her students. Later, when I was stationed at Fort Jackson, I ran into her at the bus station. She looked good, was well-dressed, and wore a big hat. She also took me out to dinner a few times. I did not keep up with her after the war.

My mother had a plot containing two rows of narcissus with a walkway down the middle. She planted a few other things, I suppose. I remember helping with weeding and getting tired before all the weeding got done. My grandmother took on milking the cow twice a day and looking after her by turning her out in the pasture.

The family compound was a busy place, especially with all the different mills in operation. As you approached our place from Highway 27, there was a dirt road that split at least 100 yards from the house. The right fork went past the impressive residence, and the left fork led to a bridge over what would come to be called Storey's Mill Creek. A wooden dam spanned the creek, and all the businesses were clustered around this area.

The house was really beautiful, with long windows and a porch wrapping around it. The porch was ten feet deep, and it attached completely on three sides and perhaps on sixty percent of the fourth side. There were two kitchen doors on the back corner facing the spring, where we got our water. The view from the kitchen was toward the creek and then north toward the spring and the larger "clubhouse." There were steps leading down to the dirt road. The view to the dam, grist mill, and sawmill was down a rather steep rocky hill. Below, a wooden boat was tied up, where my brother and I could be found playing along the creek bank. In hot weather we would put watermelons in the creek to keep them cool. I can remember sometimes seeing jugs of milk cooling in the creek, even though I don't remember if we had a milk cow.

There were a lot of people who lived at our house from time to time. When it turned out that our rural school could not house the teachers who came to teach, we took them in. There were twenty-six people besides my grandmother and my aunt and the four of us in my immediate family that I can remember who came to live with us. Mother and Dad were so kind to these folks, feeding them, providing shelter and friendship, and so forth. The most we had was four, maybe five, at any one time. Sometimes my brother and I would have to sleep in the cotton bin if we had too many people visiting our house. My parents never sent anyone away if there was work that needed to be done.

In order to accommodate the demand, we had to keep adding on to our house. We wound up with six bedrooms. My brother and I shared a bed in the corner of one room even though we were almost teenagers. That was also before we had indoor plumbing or electricity. Later on, when my parents had schoolteachers living with us, we did a pretty good job of finishing out the upstairs. We had the start of a stairway leading upstairs, but it ended in empty space and came straight down into the living room. We adapted it later on when we expanded the house in 1949 by enclosing the wide porch, living room, dining room, and one bedroom. I was a part of all the planning because I was back home from Europe by then. My parents wanted repairs done, and they were delighted that I was able to take on this project.

Highway 27 was, at least in our county, a dirt road. It was a major north/south route. Many people from Chicago, Detroit, and surrounding areas drove past our little community in huge cars. They were on their way to buy land in Florida during the boom times of the 1920s. But when the depression hit, many of these lots lost their value. Bankruptcy was common, and all those people who had driven south lost their money and their cars. They had to walk back north to what had been their homes. Whole families would be walking back north, and often they would stop by our house, which was right alongside the highway, to see if we had a drink of water or food. At that time we didn't have running water, and we'd have to carry it from the spring, which was 200 yards away. My folks knew these people were hungry as well. My mother never failed to give them a good, nourishing meal; many times she would let them sleep either on the side porch or in the corn crib.

Being around animals on the farm taught me much about life. I was fascinated with the cows, especially when it was time for one to deliver a calf. We knew it was time for a cow to be born when the cow wouldn't show up at the usual feeding place. The cows always chose the same general spot to deliver their calves—behind a pond we had on the property. I can still remember finding the mother cow and her little staggering calf already standing up or being kind of pushed up by the mother's nose. The calves would immediately start looking for food. You could tell they found nursing pretty soothing. My dad would pick up the calf in his arms and take it back to the barn. I was just so impressed by that scene. It reminded me of a Christmas card.

My family was always interested in what I did and the good and bad experiences that would shape my life forever. Every once in a while, the subject of war would come up, and my dad would ask all kinds of questions. Looking back on those days, I think he understood and anticipated the importance of coming to terms with the horrible reality of war that is thrust on very young men. Most soldiers return to "civilian life" with family and friends who cannot imagine the reality of war, and that life can seem boring in comparison.

The College Years

I was within two weeks of starting college when Germany invaded Poland. This news spread like wildfire, and for several weeks you could hear about it in conversation, in the newspaper, and every night on the radio. At the time we did not know why this happened. It was not until after the war that we actually knew the specifics of Germany's invasion.

The Nazis had been planning for quite some time to invade Poland. However, Hitler had to first make it look as though the Polish had made an offensive attack against Germany. Now famously known as the Gleiwitz incident, the Germans attacked their own radio station, posing as Polish nationals. They crossed over into Poland and killed some uniformed Polish guards. Their bodies were brought back to Germany and placed in positions to appear as if they had come across to attack the radio station. These attackers took pictures after shooting bullet holes in the station building.

After lengthy preparation, Adolf Hitler and the Nazis invaded Poland the next morning following the Gleiwitz incident. Although there were several other covert operations like the Gleiwitz incident, the Gleiwitz is the best-known event used as a catalyst to start the outbreak of war. Details of the Gleiwitz incident did not emerge until much later, toward the end of the war.

As a veteran of World War I, my father had been paying attention to Hitler's exploits and by 1939 was very interested because he knew the possible outcome of the Gleiwitz incident. In fact, he played a large part in helping me get ready for my own experience overseas. I remember frequently thinking of all the people who had lived near me in northwest Georgia who had experienced WWI, which was only twenty-eight years prior.

From reading about and hearing stories of my father's time overseas, I knew that we all should worry and fear Hitler's advance wherever he went. My father was speaking from experience, as he knew the worst part of the infantry, having served in the Meuse-Argonne offensive as an ambulance driver.

There was no question that when I went to college, I would try to participate in the Reserve Officers Training Corp (ROTC). As were most parents, my father was concerned for my safety as it looked like I would be going to Europe. More importantly, he recognized my patriotism and loyalty and the importance of the discipline and respect that the military engenders in people.

I loved wearing the uniform. I loved seeing the uniform really well-kept. I liked the discipline. I didn't like arrogance in anybody in charge of other people. I was trying to live as if there was absolutely no one beneath me. I followed something someone once said: "The only time you should look down at anybody is when he needs your help to get up." I still try to live every day like that.

I arrived at the University of Georgia on my seventeenth birthday, September 21, 1939. Upon enrolling in the University of Georgia, I joined the ROTC. I made this decision largely to try to make sure I could stay in college long enough to finish and maybe get a commission. I didn't realize at the time that the most dangerous job in the military was a junior officer in the infantry.

On Sunday, December 7, 1941, during my junior year, I was leaving the Alpha Tau Omega fraternity house when Richard Jockens ran downstairs with the news: The "Japs" were bombing our ships in Pearl Harbor! Believe it or not, there were a lot of people, including myself, who didn't know where Pearl Harbor was. Word spread slowly through the grapevine. I was not even aware that Japan was a threat. I remember people talking about how we kept sending scrap metal to Japan for a long time before this attack. I knew we would most likely be at the forefront of the whole inevitable war, and the knowledge began to sink in.

I remember thinking of everyone who had experienced the Roaring Twenties and were still trying to survive the hardships of the Great Depression. I hoped they would be able to live their lives in peace. I remember being distressed when I thought about the families who had recently experienced war in their towns and villages. I knew there were kids and teenagers trying to grow up in a peaceful world that did not exist. From the stories I heard from my father, I knew that peace would prevail, possibly a result of the optimism and resilience that only a teenager has.

Some of the people in my fraternity had already left to join the service, so that in itself gave us a little more knowledge about what was going on. I caught myself having confidence that we would win. The sad fact was that most of us did not realize just how much the members of the U.S. military would sacrifice to weather this "gathering storm."

The University of Georgia had already decided to graduate our class of 1943 in December 1942. This would allow ROTC members to head immediately to Fort Benning for a full course of Officer Candidate School (OCS). The Georgia Bulldogs had gone to their very first Rose Bowl game on January 1, 1943. I had hoped, since I had graduated early, that I might be able to go to the Rose Bowl game before I reported to Fort Benning. My father also wanted me to do that, but there was no way that even the servicemen could be guaranteed to get back to report to Fort Benning on the morning of January 3.

If you were in the four-year ROTC program at the University of Georgia, between the third and fourth year you went to the military camp. That made it possible to graduate as a second lieutenant, an officer. However, in the accelerated program, they knew we had to get there as soon as we could. We were required to take the full course load and enough other courses during the summer so we could graduate in December, six months early.

That made it necessary to go to Fort Benning and go through the OCS. Half of the men in OCS were college kids, and the other half were people who had come from the enlisted ranks. Having the enlisted men there with us made it tough, but we were all in the same boat. It was a great advantage to have respect for them and made it possible for them to respect us. The physical training was very tough. We used to say sometimes that combat would be better, but we were wrong about that, of course. Later, during combat, we realized just how important the physical training was.

There were thirty-one of us in the same ROTC class who went to OCS and fought. As far as I know, our class from Georgia had the biggest percentage of casualties. There were another thirty that went to the University of Iowa, and the other 200 were people from the enlisted ranks. A lot of people thought that would be "big-time trouble," but it was the common denominator.

I graduated from Officer Candidate School at Fort Benning on April 7, 1943. As an honor graduate, I was offered an Army commission and sent to Fort Jackson on April 17 as a replacement second lieutenant. There was a massive preparation underway for the military operation that would soon commence on the beaches of Normandy. I spent the better part of a year training with the newly established 106th Infantry Division until January 1944.

I was originally signed with the A Company, a rifle platoon, as it's called. I was approached by a man in the B Company who said that he was paired with another man he knew from college. They fussed a lot at each other, so he asked me if I would switch companies. Watching them fuss was like watching roosters fight on the farm when I was little. I agreed and took Company B.

The division was filled with kids who came as a result of lowering the draft age to eighteen. We had a lot of young high school football players. There were several close friends who were in the same class at Fort Benning as I, some of whom had been privates for a couple years and some who had family members who were already officers in the military. A couple of them had assignments to Fort Jackson.

In early January 1944, the whole division was ordered to Tennessee Maneuvers Area, which was also tough physically and tough weather-wise, especially in the wintertime. Utilized as a training area in Middle Tennessee, the Tennessee Maneuvers Area was selected because its terrain matched that of Belgium, France, and Germany. Nearly 850,000 soldiers trained there during this time.

For nearly three months, we trained under different simulated scenarios similar to the conflicts that would take place overseas. Each scenario started on a Sunday afternoon and would continue until the end of the week. We trained under thirteen different simulated scenarios over the course of thirteen weeks. When a scenario was tactical, we were to treat surrounding towns as German towns. We had many rules we were to follow to realistically replicate the European conditions.

Some of the rules prevented us from using civilian cars or entering civilian homes.

During one of these training maneuvers, we were in South Carolina. This particular scenario required us to go without food and shelter for long periods of time. It was very dark, and we were not allowed to have any artificial light. The soldiers who smoked were not even allowed to light cigarettes. We had ridden on one of the trucks for quite some time and then parked somewhere to wait for further action or instruction. It was very cold and completely miserable. In the distance we saw an old farmhouse. It must have been due to the darkness of that night, but that farmhouse was the brightest looking thing we had ever seen. All of us were starving. Some of my guys went over and knocked on the door. The nice family who lived there got busy and cooked extra biscuits and helped any way that they could.

We were not breaking any rules when it came to asking civilians for food, although it was strongly discouraged. The training at the Tennessee Maneuvers Area prepared us well, as there were times in combat when you did not see anything to eat for two or three days. We actually encountered a similar situation soon after entering Germany. Some of the German civilians would help us out, but you never knew which ones would. A lot of the civilians would make themselves known and provide what they could. It was always nice when we came across a bottle of wine. When there was a break in action or we had some downtime in quiet German towns, some guys would find stores and bum or buy candy. In several instances we came across stores filled with German jams and jellies. Even the smallest amount of nourishment after days without food makes a world of difference.

After Tennessee I went with the 106th to Camp Atterbury, located in Edinburgh, Indiana. Camp Atterbury's primary mission was to continue the training of the U.S. Army between 1942 and 1944. Wakeman Hospital Center was a 6,000-bed hospital located at the camp that trained medical professionals and treated over 85,000 patients during the war.

I borrowed the family car to drive up to Camp Atterbury. I used it to drive my supply sergeant up there. A supply sergeant serves as the custodian of arms for the division. He needed to find a place to take his wife and three kids to stay. We went to a USO dance celebration for enlisted men only, which meant I would not be allowed to go in there. The hostess sat outside and invited me to sit out there with her and watched the crowd come and go.

When my supply sergeant and I got ready to go, she asked, "Well, are you just going to live at the camp?" I replied, "I'm single and would at least like to find a place to go on the weekends." She said that her daughter and son-in-law had just left her house and that she would give me a key and invited me to come over there whenever I wanted! I did go and use the room once or twice. This is not the kind of thing that usually happens to guys in the military, but that is just how her family was!

My time at Camp Atterbury was strictly infantry troop training. This was a time that we strengthened our endurance. It was unknown how long we would be walking in Europe. Some thought we would ride all the way, and others predicted we would walk hundreds of miles. The second guy was quite a bit more accurate. This was also a great time for bonding.

Relationships and friendships are the most precious of bonds in wartime. This is a theme that I will repeat many times in these pages. I started to understand the meaning of real relationships. The reason I wound up with many friends and close companions was because I had the same platoon three different times: at Fort Jackson, Tennessee Maneuvers, and then later at Camp Atterbury. I always made it a point to be the friend and give orders in such a way that did not demean anybody. This feeling continued to grow and was especially true as I experienced the war in Metz, a small town in Germany.

The symbol on your shoulder was always analyzed by your comrades. It signified the battalion you were in and where you would be deployed. When someone you cared about was ordered somewhere very dangerous, you immediately tried to find out if they were okay.

Journey to Europe

May 1944 began with orders to report to Camp Shanks in Orangetown, New York, a small town just outside of New York City.

I had four days before I had to show up, and I knew I wanted to use this time to go home, so I called my mother and told her I wanted to come home for four days. Her first response was "Why?" It was almost as if she knew there had to be a reason for a spontaneous four-day break. It was then that I was given the news that I was to report to Camp Shanks.

I traveled back home and was able to spend time with my family for four days. I drove the family car back to Rome from Fort Atterbury, which was about a ten-hour drive from what I remember. There's no good way to describe goodbyes. I spent as much time with my parents as I could. It was somewhat of a solemn time, because there was no guarantee that I would return home.

The military had informed us of the different ways we could get to Fort Shanks. I took a bus. On the way to Camp Shanks, I stopped at Fort Belvoir in Fairfax County, Virginia, where I visited my brother for one night, eventually arriving at Camp Shanks around May 31.

Camp Shanks, "Last Stop, USA," near New York City, was the largest point of embarkation for most of the soldiers and troops headed to the front lines in North Africa and Europe. Nearly 1.5 million soldiers (almost 40,000 per month) were issued combat equipment and conducted final inspections. I spent ten days at Camp Shanks.

Camp Shanks was a place to deal with life in its most serious moments, to deal with the need to be honest with myself and with my family and friends. We had to come to terms with the fact that many of us would be killed. I made conversations with family and friends frequently while at Camp Shanks. I remember that I always wanted to be able to get leave and talk to my parents. Talking to your family was rare, but when you did have the chance, you would have to tell them that when you received new orders, you would not be able to talk to them anymore. You kept repeating that until it was true.

Every morning, we were called to calisthenics at 8:00 AM. When the calisthenics were over, we were released until the next morning at 8:00 AM. Between our other preparations and inspections, this left us with quite a bit of free time.

In the first couple of hours I was in the camp, I overheard people talking about exploring New York City. Over the course of the next ten days, we explored many areas of the city and even went to some Broadway shows! There were always people standing out with tickets to give to servicemen.

One time, an aunt of mine from Chattanooga had taken me to New York to the World's Fair, where I had seen the Billy Rose Aquacade. Billy Rose was known for the spectacular shows that he could produce. On one of the last few nights at Camp Shanks, four of us non-drinking farm guys decided to go into the city together. We had been to several clubs like the Stork Club, but this time I suggested that we go to the Diamond Horseshoe, a big night club owned by Billy Rose. I knew the names of the places to go but had never been there myself. We four ordered a claret lemonade and decided that was enough for four.

A "cigarette girl" approached our table. I playfully remarked to one of the guys that I thought she was so beautiful that, if she touched me, I might melt. Some of the other boys told her to come and touch me. I asked for her number, but she said she couldn't give it to me. However, one of the boys slipped me a piece of paper later. On it was her phone number!

She went by the name of Melody Tome. At the end of her shift, around 2:00 AM, she met me, and we walked for miles and miles, stopping at famous night clubs, my uniform being respected wherever we went. One visit was to the Stork Club, a place I had long ago read about. We were escorted to a corner table in the dining room and welcomed by a gentleman who turned out to be the owner. Shortly, a waiter came with champagne, and I tried to explain that there was a mistake. "Compliments of Mr. Billingsley," he explained. Then came a small bottle of perfume for "the lady."

Melody was very smart and became one of those people you count on to remember. Her real name was actually Dottie, but she was unable to go by this name for safety concerns. Several more dates ensued, for which I was most grateful. She was staying at Barbizon for Women, where men were not allowed past the front desk. My brother even saw her a few times on his way to the Pacific as an engineer. Her dad was in the military somewhere. She was very unusual in that she never wanted to go to bed with anybody. She was just paying her own bills and making her own way.

I explained that one day soon I would not be able to tell her where I would be going and that I would probably never see her again. On one of our last dates, we saw from Times Square that the D-Day landings had taken place. That close to the invasion, there were people who were excited about it. There is a famous picture of the sailor and the nurse. It was that kind of celebratory atmosphere. I was not the least bit afraid. We were committed to the war and committed to doing the right thing. The military was accepted as being the force that would save our skins.

My recollection is that we left from New York to Europe on the night of June 8, 1944, as passengers on a banana boat built in 1918 that belonged to the United Fruit Line. The Allies made use of nearly every kind of seaworthy vessel during the war. One can only imagine the thousands of soldiers and the tons and tons of equipment and machines that crossed the oceans.

We were in a convoy of fifty ships with the destination of Greenock, Scotland. We numbered about 200 passengers—all of us were officers, first and second lieutenants—all of us sailing into an experience for which none of us could truly be prepared.

We quickly realized that sardines would have felt right at home. We were housed in "state rooms," each with two upper and two lower bunks. We barely had room to lay a small suitcase between bunks in order to play cards. Each of the four of us had to get out of bed one at a time.

The ship ahead of us was a Norwegian ammunition ship whose captain suffered from poor eyesight. He was afraid he was going to hit the boat ahead of him and kept lagging back. One morning we awoke, and out of the original fifty ships, we could only see three other ships near us. With only four ships in our convoy now, we were very vulnerable to any attack.

There were other smaller ships, classified as corvettes, which were used for antisubmarine defense. The folks in charge knew they were taking a chance by putting so many of us on the ship to Europe. For twenty-four hours we were separated from the main convoy of ships. The corvettes circled our four ships, frequently dropping depth bombs in order to protect us from German U-boats. All of this was a bit unnerving, and we were on edge until we caught up to the main convoy of ships. We were definitely relieved to reach port and get our feet back on solid ground.

It took us sixteen days after departing from New York to arrive in Greenock, Scotland. From there we boarded the train and headed to Audlem in midwestern England. We were not allowed to leave, except to go to the pub and to get physical exams. We were there for two or three weeks for training.

From there we boarded a train and headed south to Southampton. By then I had a promotion to first lieutenant. Somewhere in England I had another physical, and a medical officer said, "Hey, Lieutenant, did you know you are flat-footed? We can call this a disability, and I can keep you in England!" Yes, I knew it, but staying there was not what I trained for, and they needed first lieutenants badly. My feet had been tested on the farm in Chattooga County, in Athens, Fort Benning, Fort Jackson, at Tennessee Maneuvers, at Camp Atterbury—and walking a beautiful date home late at night for the few nights I could get a pass from Camp Shanks.

July 9, 1944:
Normandy and Utah Beach

In Southampton, an Indian ship was waiting to take us across the English Channel to France. On that last night I didn't know where we were, just that we were miles from the English Channel. I spent the night in some vast building among a throng of people.

Before boarding the ship, all of the soldiers were very quiet. As we boarded, a fellow was looking at a list and slapping a Red Diamond patch on the shoulders of various guys. He'd call out, "Red Diamond Division, Priority Level." We were referred to as the Red Diamond group of junior officers. The Red Ball Express was Hitler's highway transport system to Normandy, which became an asset for us as we swiftly moved past the Normandy beaches.

"Priority level" meant we would be sent into the heart of the fighting, where it was expected we would experience a pretty high casualty count. When we first started, we figured that we were of a higher status, meaning we would be able to take cover behind a tree or a wall or something and not be at the forefront of the fighting. But, of course, we were quite wrong about that.

I boarded the ship with about 250 junior officers. As far as any of us knew, we were part of a "replacement package" in the 5th Infantry Division before the formation of Patton's famous Third Army.

A few clouds were floating along the bleak pathless sky and the stillness of the day was marked by the rumble of hovering planes overhead and artillery in the distance.[1]

The morning light revealed a fleet of all kinds of watercraft, each with a barrage balloon moored via a cable to prevent strafing by the enemy. Attached to the balloon were heavy cables that created a difficult approach to a low-flying aircraft. We received orders to transfer from the Indian ship onto a landing craft infantry (LCI). These were smaller boats that were very low to the water and had a door on the front that lowered so we could easily run off and onto the beach.

Transfer from the larger boat proved challenging as the very large waves caused the LCI to move up and down about five feet. You had to balance on the larger ship and jump to the LCI when the timing was right. It also did not help that it was very early in the morning and quite hard to see. As the LCI and the larger ship scraped together, one soldier crushed his ankle between the watercraft. His time in Europe was short, and he did not even make it to the beach. Another soldier lost his balance and dropped his rifle into the ocean.

As the LCI took off, we shortly were able to see Utah Beach.

The choppy waters of the channel slashed against the shores that still showed signs of the greatest landing operation in war history. Broken and half-sunken ships dotting the water and beaches. But also on those shores were ships and landing craft unloading precious cargo of men and war supplies. Not far from the shores a high, steep hill could be seen that shadowed the inland view. And into that shadow was moving the 5th Division, which not long after deemed itself to be one of the war's famous.[2]

About 200 yards from the beach, I heard one of the guys yell, "This is really it, guys!" The ramp attached to the front of the LCI dropped in about two and a half feet of water. They marched you off in the water about waist deep. We were at Utah Beach. As my feet touched the sand, I began to have serious thoughts of people and home and the odds of seeing them again.

On the afternoon of July 9, the company landed with six officers and 137 enlisted men. They moved inland for several miles to an assembly area where they bivouacked for the night.[3]

Between the hedgerows, the commanding officers counted people with no records or anything and divided us into different groups. Apparently, they had been told to get as many junior officers over to Normandy as necessary and that further orders and assignments would be made after we arrived. We were put in different divisions depending on the number of casualties that we were replacing. We were told to gather up our groups in the dark.

I did some patrolling, and later that night I became first lieutenant leader of Company C, 10th Infantry, 5th Division. Some guy came over and got me and was wondering what kind of lieutenant they were getting that evening.

The size of Company C was a little over 200. Several of my new comrades began to pick on me for my age. I was the youngest in the group. They frequently commented that I looked about fifteen years old and that if I survived a week with my platoon, I would probably be all right. I did in fact survive my first week and was one of only two people who survived six months after our landing at Utah Beach.

"Two days later the company encamped near Vacquerie after an eighteen-mile hike through shattered countryside."[4]

Notes

[1] *The History of Company C, 10th Infantry U.S. Inf. Fifth Division, in the Battle of Europe*, 2. Several sections of a piece titled *The History of Company C, 10th Infantry U.S. Inf. Fifth Division, in the Battle of Europe* have been included to help "fill in the gaps" between Mr. Storey's stories. Lt. Robert Dunn worked closely with Mr. Storey and several other members of the company shortly after the war to compile and write *The History of Company C*. This piece tells the complete history of Mr. Storey's company during the war and gives a thorough overview, locations, and dates that correspond with Mr. Storey's retellings. *The History of Company C* was never published and was only used as a reference between the veterans of Company C after the war.

[2] Ibid.
[3] Ibid.
[4] Ibid., 3.

July 26, 1944: Vidouville

The troops were adjusting themselves to conditions for the first ten days, taking up defensive positions.[1]

Hedgerows are well-grown edges of fields. The roads were little farm tracks that had been worn deeper into the earth over the centuries. This caused the hedgerows to be very tall and make excellent cover. However, anywhere you were, there were Germans close who were also using the hedgerows for their protection.

After taking our defensive positions on my first day, the company commander sent me out on a patrol. I was so much younger and less experienced than he was, so I took a couple guys with me. I was in front, and we were supposed to discover just how close the Germans were. Part of determining this was to draw fire, which meant we had to shoot our guns randomly to see if somebody shot back. From that we could determine where the enemy was and just how much resistance we were facing.

I was crawling along one side of the hedgerows when suddenly I heard German being spoken on the other side, probably ten feet away. We stopped crawling and flattened ourselves on the ground. I heard an explosion and felt real pain and numbness on my backside. I had two grenades in my pockets, which I removed in order to be even lower to the ground. My first thought was, "How am I going to tell my father that I got hit in the behind my first patrol!" I felt back there and discovered that I wasn't bleeding.

It turned out that we had been hit by a little concussion grenade, a common weapon carried by many German soldiers. Concussion grenades are filled with air, not like a shrapnel grenade. They are activated by tapping them on your helmet and then tossed in the desired direction. The explosion was meant to be more psychological than anything. It worked for a little bit. I found out later that the grenade had knocked a piece of bark off a tree, which then hit me in the behind. I had no million-dollar wound, just pain and embarrassment.

The first prisoners taken by the company were credited to PFC Claude Nolan, who caught the two German soldiers on that patrol near the company lines.[2]

For a few days, we were in sort of a stable situation, so we did more patrolling. At one point I took a couple guys and climbed over a fence. That's when I saw my first dead body, a paratrooper who looked to be from the All-American Division. I wondered how he was killed. It occurred to me that he was wearing leggings, not boots. The leggings had a buckle on them. Apparently the buckle on the paratrooper's leggings had caught a booby trap cord, which initiated the explosion. As I jumped over the fence, I found the spent booby trap. If I had been the first over the fence, then I would have been the one who set off the booby trap! My patrol proceeded into the pasture area. There were a lot of cows but no Germans on that particular trip.

Finding fresh water was a big concern. We found some water where we could fill our canteens and use our Halazone tablets (water purification tablets), which I suggested we do. After our canteens were filled, we went a little further upstream and were astonished to discover a dead cow lying across the stream, with the water pouring over the cow. We questioned whether or not to throw out the water we had just filled our canteens with, but we decided that if we used our Halazone tablets, we should be okay.

On the morning of July 30, just a few days after being relieved by a Scottish Infantry unit, the company fought in the battle of Hill 183. Enemy resistance was stiff, and the fire was severe, but the troops held their ground and also turned back a German counterattack which came at night. Although only a short time in combat, the troops conducted themselves as veterans. The character, patience, and fortitude were to be more than thoroughly tried in the months ahead than they have been in the time spent since coming overseas. What they saw was only a preview of coming events. Victory was to be gradual: the fighting hard and no emotionalism shown toward the gangsters of Hitler. There was a wave of confidence over the troops as they found themselves on French soil and taking part in this gigantic operation. But there was also disillusion as the men saw the actual results of the German-occupied empire: a people living in hunger and misery. It wasn't a reality anymore. It was a real war against a stubborn enemy.[3]

Notes

[1] *The History of Company C, 10th Infantry U.S. Inf. Fifth Division, in the Battle of Europe*, 3.

[2] Ibid.

[3] Ibid.

August 9–10, 1944: Saint-Lo and Angers

We were able to watch from some distance back the bombing of St. Lo, which was destroyed.

But that made possible a swift and convincing drive following the break-through at St. Lo. It sent the Germans reeling back, making them groggy and even jittery from the lightning blows as the divisions on the spearhead pushed the Germans across France.[1]

The Third Army had been formed in July, and we were transferred over to it from the First Army. Under orders from Patton, we then began a trek of walking and hitching rides on all sorts of vehicles, each day wondering which was the worst demise: fatigue or bullets.

Infantry units didn't have enough vehicles to transport all the troops, so we were ordered to jump on any vehicle we came across. During World War II there was a lot of ride hitching on artillery battalion vehicles or tank battalion vehicles. Sometimes this included command jeeps, messenger cars, and every now and then a motorcycle. We didn't use any motorcycles often, but the Germans did.

From the bomb-leveled town of St. Lo, the troops moved through Coutances, Avranches, and La Guerche, taking prisoners as they went along.[2]

I gained command of the 2nd Platoon of the 1st Battalion of the 10th Infantry which was a part of the 5th Infantry Division. With this position came a new level of responsibility. Most of the soldiers knew a commander had to possess both authority and the ability to clearly convey orders. It was of paramount importance that the guys under my command understood the reasons for the orders. The guys simply had to have respect for the one who was telling them what they had to do. There was no question about that. I also had to establish relation-ships with all my men. Many of our friendships have now survived for seventy-five years. It is not enough just to be an authority; there must also be respect and feelings of friendship, no matter how tough the combat is.

My unit was in a convoy that passed through St. Lo and headed toward a town called Avranche, which is almost inside Mont St. Michel. At that point, we realized there was a lot of air activity in the area. The Allies had air superiority by then. We found out later how close the Germans had come to cutting us off. They were within sight of Mont St. Michel when we were passing through. The Air Force is responsible for cutting that off (in addition to the 30th Division, which has been written about in a book called *Mortagne*, a little village they were able to hold). It was a key operation for the Germans to keep us out, so they made many attempts to do so. The Germans announced that our Air Force that day seriously wounded General Rommel, the famous German general. They announced another day that he had died as a result of it. It wasn't until much later that we found out that the Germans had made him commit suicide.

After making it through Avranche, we then branched out for a number of days. Sometimes we were able to hop on vehicles and ride, but mostly we walked toward Lyon and Le Mans. Le Mans was a place we had actually heard of because of the famous automobile races.

On the 10th of August the company was in the battle for Angers. Before reaching the town a river had to be crossed. Although the bridge was found intact, the Germans made suicide attempts to destroy it before the oncoming troops. Loaded down with explosives, the Germans came within fifteen yards of the bridge, but the attack was broken up and the [Allied] men moved into the town and then secured a chateau on the outskirts of Angers. Among the booty found in the former German headquarters were numerous cases of champagne, more than enough for the troops.[3]

Notes

[1] *The History of Company C, 10th Infantry U.S. Inf. Fifth Division, in the Battle of Europe*, 3.

[2] Ibid., 3–4.

[3] Ibid., 4.

August 18, 1944: Chartres

After traveling eighty miles through dust and hot sun, riding everything from jeeps to artillery pieces in an effort to keep at the heels of the retreating Germans, the company reached St. Calais on August 13. They occupied Thivars, Montainville, and on August 18 set up a defense on the outskirts of Chartres. Elements of the Third Army, including the XX Corps and my unit, were based just outside the historic town of Chartres, southwest of Paris. In August 1944, General George S. Patton's Third Army awaited orders to take Paris—orders that would never come.

I was amazed to find myself in France but dismayed by the circumstances that had brought me there. In Chartres, I found myself stationed close enough to the great cathedral to be able to see one of the rose windows! The experience was all so surreal to me. I was proud to be a part of the effort to take the town and thus secure it from Nazi occupation. Part of that effort included destroying Chartres because of information leading the Allies to believe German soldiers were hiding in the cathedral. I had long been intrigued by Chartres Cathedral and the architectural history of France, especially as it relates to her great cathedrals.

It wasn't until long after the war that I learned an American Army officer who was part of the effort to take Chartres challenged the orders to destroy the cathedral and thus spared it from destruction. His name was Col. Wellborn Barton Griffith of Texas, logistics and liaison officer in the XX Corps. In mid-August, he found out we had orders to bomb Chartres Cathedral in order to defeat German snipers who were thought to be hiding in its towers. Earlier, many precautions were taken to preserve as much of the cathedral as possible. Almost all of the original artwork and beautiful stained glass had been removed and stored somewhere, knowing the cathedral would be vulnerable to attacks.

Even though the Germans still occupied the city of Chartres, Col. Griffith challenged the order of destroying the cathedral. He volunteered to go behind enemy lines and inspect the cathedral to see if any German snipers were indeed camping out in its towers. Griffith entered and inspected the cathedral but found no Germans. After returning and reporting his findings, the order to destroy the cathedral was canceled, and the Allies liberated the area shortly after. He is credited for saving the Cathedral of Notre-Dame de Chartres.

After the orders were canceled, Griffith resumed his mission to liberate the city. Suddenly, he encountered nearly fifteen of the enemy and retreated to the nearest Allied outpost, where he found a tank. The Allies began a counterattack after Griffith directed them to where he had encountered Germans. During the attack, the Allies were exposed to heavy fire. It was here that Griffith was killed.

Local residents saw him fall and within hours had covered him with flowers and an American flag. A plaque now stands where Griffith was killed, and he was posthumously awarded the Distinguished Cross, Silver Star, Purple Heart, Legion of Merit, and the French Croix de Guerre and the Legion d'Honneur.

Another chapter in the history of the cathedral ended with the fall of Griffith. Throughout history, fires and other "acts of God" have threatened the cathedral, but it still stands today.

It wasn't until long after WWII that I was able to revisit this area as a tourist. I had learned more about the impressive history of Chartres in the years after the war ended, which made me even more grateful to have been a part of the Allied effort to keep the great church from further harm.

August 24, 1944: Fontainebleau, Seine, and Montereau

With the resistance being light, the mad dash across France kept up its fast pace.

The next objectives of the Red Diamonds were Etamps, south of Paris, and Fontainebleau, sixty miles distant on the Seine River. They then proceeded to Montereau, seventy-two miles away, where they occupied positions. These movements, when completed, would enable the Third Army to outflank Paris and sever northern France from southern France.[1]

We traveled quickly in this particular area. We were trying to catch up with the Germans, and occasionally we did. We were always at their heels, always stopping at a village that was just across the road from where they were. They had to use whatever they had to resist us. We used a lot of artillery, and we were free to do it simply because many of the towns had been evacuated, but occasionally we came across people who never left.

Shortly after approaching Montereau, we came upon a gorgeous house overlooking the Seine River. A very frightened elderly lady lived there by herself. She had heard bombing and artillery every night for a long time. For three or four years, she had been sleeping in a chair in her basement! She begged me to tell her that she would be safe to sleep in the main part of the house. I told her, "I cannot tell you that because you will still hear all of the bombing and artillery. You will probably be safer if you stay in the basement. It's going to be this way for a while. Some of that artillery is ours."

These situations were especially difficult because we witnessed first-hand the fear of the innocent, of a people who never asked to be involved in this war or to be exposed to this kind of danger.

Since we were in Montereau, the Germans attempted to "disguise" themselves on the radio by putting on "American accents" and cutting into our frequencies to talk about baseball statistics. I guess they thought they could fool us into giving them intel by knowing who won the World Series. This didn't work on us. By cutting into our frequency, we were able to tell where they were. I mentioned over the air that we knew where they were, and one of the Germans cussed me out for everything in the world. He had even learned all of the American cuss words.

Fighting a war with the purpose of defending half the world is a humanizing thing. Within you is the empathy that makes you want to do the right thing, which is to stop it. A lot of times we took prisoners and had orders to use our ammunition on them. We didn't have enough people to evacuate prisoners, but we didn't want to kill them. I never did comply with that order. I don't know anyone who did.

Many times throughout the war, we were hard pressed for people. About three months after the invasion, we were getting so many guys who hadn't had much training. We had one particular captain who took my place who had come from a camp in Georgia. This particular captain didn't know how to use the radio, and he was with me all the time. At one point, I managed to get my radio set up while we were in a pretty good-sized depression. We couldn't be seen by the enemy, but we could see where the Germans were and that they were firing in our general direction. This new captain was standing on the edge of the woods and moving a squad of one of the platoons in. He had told them to "get on out there." Every one of those men got shot down. That was the night when I got a message to tell the new guy to leave his maps with me and report to battalion.

I was asked to help the battalion commander by taking a half-day to write up a report on what the new captain had done and reclassify him. At times like this, I became frustrated with the people who were placing these poorly trained soldiers. It seemed like sometimes they bent over backwards to send guys into the wrong places and get some of them killed.

I then asked the battalion executive about the transfer and what was going on, and he said, "Oh well, you're the company commander now." I responded with something like, "Okay, I've got two other guys I need to get rid of." He told me they were going to replace them, which was a favor for them because they could resign their commission or stay in the military.

I asked if there was some way I could ask the two for their resignations. He told me no, but I could give them the order to resign and, if they didn't comply, court martial them. I thought that was a terrible thing to happen to a couple pretty good guys. However, in the back of my mind, I was thinking of all the other private first class officers. I had to do what was best for all of us. I didn't always know what to do, but I knew most of the time what not to do. This I did know: It was not about feeding lives to the enemy. It was about looking after our guys the best I possibly could and using their skills. I knew they could only perform their best if they were being led right; so began my mission.

During my first few weeks as company commander, I had a couple of kids just lose their marbles. As a means to escape, one platoon leader shot his hand with his .45 pistol. He didn't have to come back. Another officer who was terrified came up to me crying, "I can't do it; I can't do it!" Shortly after I helped him calm down, he placed his M-1 rifle on top of his foot and pulled the trigger. These were counted as casualties, and they were sent home. This was all very challenging, but we had to push forward.

As we continued to move through France, we directed our artillery to try to maneuver in such a way as to control the movement of the Germans. We had been pushing across France so fast that sometimes you would find a small group of Germans who didn't want to do much resisting.

Most of the towns and villages were evacuated, but in some of them a few people remained. One beautiful village on a hill suddenly burst out with firepower as the Germans had found good visibility of our approach. We stopped and took what protection was available and ordered artillery fire. Our version of the 105mm howitzer was, unfortunately, inferior to the German 88, which had the muzzle velocity of a rifle. That was why they could even snipe. It took two days before we were able to approach from a different direction. This delay made it possible for many of the remaining Germans to escape.

One of the Germans' defenses was to take the refugees and force them west across France toward us, effectively using them as a shield. The refugees traveled by horse and pushcart. I don't remember seeing any bicycles, but they used anything else that would roll. Every now and then we would find someone who had been hurt by our own bombing. In the rubble of one little town a couple of adults emerged from the rubble with a little girl about ten years of age, who had an infected arm. Our medics looked after and treated her wounds. The artillery I had ordered earlier had wounded her forearm. My innate pacifism was renewed with the realization that the innocent suffer the most.

It was increasingly difficult every time I saw people so mistreated by the enemy. The Germans continued to insist that the civilians should evacuate toward us, which would put them in the middle of the fighting. As a result, a lot of people were killed. It was difficult to pass them alongside the road with horse-drawn carriages carrying everything they owned. The thousands of dead horses and cows spread across the French countryside were all that was left of the endless brutality between the lines.

After watching *Saving Private Ryan* in 1998, I was reminded of our own "Private Ryan." I received a message from Eisenhower saying to get Sgt. Petroski out of combat. He was one of four brothers, and the other three had either been seriously wounded or killed. He was taken back to regimental headquarters and left in Luxembourg. I found out after the war that he never went home, but rather remained overseas. He stayed in the rear area because he was ordered not to be in the combat area. There were seven cases like that during World War II as I understood. This was never official, a tradition rather than a requirement. That shows a little bit of heart anyway.

Note

[1] *The History of Company C, 10th Infantry U.S. Inf. Fifth Division, in the Battle of Europe*, 4.

August 30, 1944:
Marne, Reims, and Verdun

The fighting up to this time was sparse and fast. The battles were short and decisive. The Germans were on the run and had no time to set up a defense capable of stopping the American blitz. Enemy motorized battalions, infantry, and patrols were opposed by the crushing troops, but they couldn't cope with the spearhead led by the Red Diamond Division. The Maine, Seine, Marne, Vesle, and Aisne rivers were crossed with no organized enemy resistance. The troops moved fast, sometimes pushing themselves to keep going. They got their sleep from short naps while bouncing along on vehicles or hiking under the sultry summer sun and blinding rainstorms.

It was the same routine for the 700-mile dash across France. Streets of liberated towns were lined with old and young, shouting, throwing flowers, passing out drinks and fruits to the tired, bearded passing troops. Collaborators were marched down the streets followed by an angry crowd who jeered and ripped off their clothing and led them to jail—sometimes to their death. French women who had been friendly with German troops were punished by having their heads shaved in public and then marched through the streets. Little children were often seen hanging on jeeps and asking the Yanks for cigarettes and chocolate. Aged French stared at the passing troops and the unbelievable war machines. Homes were shattered from American and German shells, and livestock could be seen lying dead on the fields and streets. These were but a few of the countless scenes that took place as the American liberation troops moved on.[1]

As we continued our terrible zig-zag trip across France and into Germany, many questioned why we had to be there and what might have been if we were never there. The further we went, the more we knew that the war had to be fought to stop Hitler's promise to rule the world. Even as we saw our friends killed and wounded, we knew that we had to keep on as long as we could until the Allies were victorious.

We were soon alerted for a move to Verdun. Verdun was where, in World War I, the French had stopped the German drive. Some of us were excited to be at a place we had heard of from history books. In a peaceful setting, and weather good for a change, there were a number of comments about the fact that only twenty-five years had passed since our parents were there. My dad had driven a Model T ambulance in that area during WWI in the area. I wrote to him—maybe the only letter I had written to him directly—and said I thought I had slept in his foxhole.

The announcement came that we were very restricted in our use of vehicles because the Third Army was nearly out of gas for trucks, cooking, and delivery of food! With this came some good news: Dinah Shore would be singing for the troops at 7:00 PM at an auditorium nearby! As usual, three or four people from each unit could go, and this time company officers could attend if their units were safe for the moment.

The concert was remarkable. For two hours Dinah cupped her ear after each number to hear some favorite song mentioned and started singing the request while the accompanist listened hard in order to catch up. At the end of her concert, there was a big crowd of guys in love with Dinah Shore *and* somebody back home. After the war, I read that some general had asked that she have a concert for upper-grade officers only. Dinah told him that she had come to sing for the "troops"!

But soon that brief rest was to come to an end. The battles that followed were to be hard, dragged-out affairs. The weather was becoming unfavorable for combat, and along with the rain and mud, progress was slowed because of supplies. Dust came from the abrupt ending of the race across France, mainly due to the gas shortage. The history of the war might have been changed if the 5th Division and the armored divisions had had enough fuel to keep them at the heels of the retreating Germans.[2]

Notes

[1] *The History of Company C, 10th Infantry U.S. Inf. Fifth Division, in the Battle of Europe*, 5.
[2] Ibid.

September 7, 1944: Preparing for Metz

The Third Army's rapid drive across France had outrun their supply lines.[1]

Patton's Third Army, the real one, wasn't formed until four or five weeks after Normandy. We were in the First Army until he came over. He said, "I thought we would wade through mud and water and were going to get to Berlin first if it took a carload of dog tags." Patton was a big talker. He was a warrior, and that's all he wanted to do. I got to be in his presence one time at a meeting. It was pretty dramatic. We were stuck in the mud in France, and he showed up. My company commander sent me to the meeting. We didn't have to dress up; we didn't have anywhere to dress up. I had never seen so much spit wash and polish as we prepared for Patton's arrival.

Patton's Jeep arrived, fishtailing like a jet ski. The road was narrow and difficult, like many French roads, and under nearly three inches of mud due to the frequent traffic. The only people with him were his driver and his aide, who was manning a fifty-caliber machine gun. Patton hopped out, wiped mud off his face with both his hands, and stood there and got very inspirational as he spoke and insisted that the Germans were more afraid of us (Fifth Division, Red Diamond) than anything else. It turns out that he told all of his troops the same thing. It was rather dramatic, but his speech left us impressed!

A resupply of ammunition and especially gasoline for the vehicles was received on September 6, which allowed the Third Army to continue its drive eastward. After the supplies caught up, the division again began its drive toward Metz. After marching several miles, the company bivouacked in the woods near Arnaville for the night.[2]

As we began traveling further toward Metz, we became encouraged by the movement we had made, as we were now about five miles away. After having traveled so fast up to this point, we had been so disappointed that we were now facing a two-month delay before we could move on to Metz. Our movement had been so fast I boasted to people that we walked, ran, and crawled across land in record time through the plains south of Paris.

General Patton gave the order that we must attack Metz. The ancient city of Metz is surrounded by more than ten forts dating back over 300 years. We did not know that the Germans had armed those forts with artillery guns on elevators that could be raised and fired from the rooftops. Our lull in activities had enabled the Germans to prepare a strong line of defense on the east side of the Moselle River. The next twenty-five days were the worst for our division in establishing a bridge head across the Moselle.

Notes

[1] *The History of Company C, 10th Infantry U.S. Inf. Fifth Division, in the Battle of Europe,* 5.

[2] Ibid.

Mid-September:
Moselle River at Dornot,
Moselle River at Arnaville,
Hill 386, Silver Star

Early in the morning on September 8, the company made a surprise crossing of the Moselle River and headed for the high ground overlooking the town of Arry.[1]

I have never written down a description of the intense fighting and heavy losses that occurred in trying to cross the Moselle River, south of Metz. The next seven days required extreme tenacity to hold this important position.

It was unusual to feel somewhat quiet in an area relatively undisturbed by our war. In the race across France, we had seen and caused much destruction of villages and countryside, and now we were faced with telling our enlisted men and junior officers that we were assigned enough vehicles to move us farther east toward Metz. There was not much to say as we got ready for this move. We were loaded on 6 x 6 trucks, followed Captain Davis's Jeep (our current company commander), and traveled to a small town which we were told was near the Moselle River.

As we approached the Metz area, only several kilometers away from the Moselle River, we got orders to make a river crossing and to attack a rather steep hill on the other side of the river. The officers cautioned the men about being very quiet as we began an almost three-hour hike. At about three or four in the morning, in complete darkness, we walked about three kilometers to where we were going to make the crossing. We moved to the marshy edge of the river. When we finally halted, word was passed that we should sit down along a somewhat improved dirt road.

We found out the river was somewhat flooded, which made it harder to operate the small boats for the crossing. Somebody found me along the column of men and told me to report to the company commander.

Captain Davis had been overseas for all this time. He was a pretty tough guy. He called for me to crawl up to where he was, standing in a little bit of water on the edge of the swollen Moselle River. He greeted me with, "Storey, I don't believe these other goddamned guys can get us across the river and up the hill" (officially Hill 386 in the history books). He said he felt this would be the toughest test we had faced. He felt at that moment my second platoon would be most likely to succeed in getting up the hill against the enemy fire we expected. He explained that two other attempts to cross the river had failed, one to the north and another to the south of us. He explained that a pontoon bridge was just being finished and that I would lead my platoon across the bridge and up the hill. We would be walking into the face of small arms fire and three or four tanks that were operating from just inside the walls of the village called Arry, which was originally thought to be abandoned by the Germans.

He was recruiting some pretty good soldiers. I was flattered, and I didn't even bat an eye. I said, "I'm ready." Captain Davis went on to explain how important the capture of Metz was to the Third Army. After crossing the river and conquering the hill, we would eventually facilitate the encircling of the city. I began to doubt my ability to effectively lead an infantry unit, given my youth, Southern drawl, and inexperience in that division.

So balanced on pontoons as makeshift boats to cross across the river, not waiting for the engineers to finish the pontoon bridge. Up to this point, the Germans could observe the pontoon bridge that the engineers would complete the next day. We began to use smoke in the daylight to try to obscure what we were doing, but every time the engineers would complete the pontoon bridge, the Germans would knock it out. Our guys would then have to build it at night to get the supplies over. You can imagine how long it took to get several tanks over to the bridge while rolling up and down both banks.

The battle for this bridgehead, in its crucial essence, is neither dramatic nor human but hell on earth. Constant enemy machine gun, mortar, and artillery fire was thrown at the attacking troops. For the first three days of the bridgehead battle, the men had to face a tank-supported enemy with only rifle fire as it was impossible to get tanks and heavy guns across the river due to the intense fire that repeatedly knocked out everything the engineers set up. Twice, the company was forced to give up the gained grounds, but the third time they charged up the hill with the command of "Fix bayonets!" and routed the Germans from their positions with the cold steel.

It was on this hill where Capt. William B. Davis, Commanding Officer, died a heroic death. After being wounded in the legs and refusing evacuation, he directed the operations from the litter but shortly after was killed when another shell hit nearby. The 6-foot, 200-pound captain was the idol of "C" Company and won the admiration and respect of everyone who knew him. Another courageous feat was that of PFC Wilbert Dodson, who killed thirty-seven German soldiers while operating the machine gun as they were charging toward the company's position. The assistance of fighter planes, although it was close-range fighting, helped considerably, along with artillery fire, in turning back enemy troops and tanks.[2]

I moved the second platoon to the river's edge with me and quietly told squad leaders we would run across the pontoon bridge with fixed bayonets and charge up open spaces of the hill screaming like crazy. As we got to the top of the hill, by afternoon we formed a rather sparse line of defense. A couple other companies joined us and added to our thin line.

We faced a lot of rifle fire and some heavier stuff from the "Arry tanks" before the German tanks moved out and obviously headed beyond the hill toward the east—except one, which tried to travel across our front with the idea of cutting off our advance. Our bazooka man had one round and fired it about forty-five degrees off target because the fins were bent! During the terrible day more people were wounded with artillery and mortar fire. Captain Davis was killed, and Lt. Dille assumed command. Later, when there was a rare delivery of mail to the company, I found out that Capt. William Davis was an Alpha Tau Omega fraternity brother.

We were ordered to get our company organized and proceed through the walls of the village of Arry, which had been evacuated, and move the two hundred or so yards to the exit from the town on the other side. The mission was to move into Arry at 3:00 AM to protect our flank before the enemy could reoccupy the village. It turned out that the

Germans had reoccupied the town pretty strongly and they killed one of the officers and wounded another one.

As our forward people moved into the town through the gate, they were immediately attacked. The company commander, Lt. Dille, was killed. The second-in-command, Lt. Cupelli, was wounded. He wasn't evacuated at first because we were under such serious fire. The medics finally got him on the litter to take him down the hill. He was killed by artillery, but they continued the evacuation of his body. We exited the town and sort of stayed along the wall until we could find out what was going on and who was left.

The people who were left moved along the village wall and stayed put until daylight, when I began assessing our situation, knowing that all the other officers' ranks were lesser than mine. The weapons platoon leader survived, and he was now in charge and was the only one who outranked me. I found him seated in part of a foxhole, scared sick from fear and told me that he couldn't go on. Therefore, I became company commander. When daylight came, I gathered up whoever I could find who was still alive. I made sure we were down close to the river staying out of enemy view. I made sure that they guys all did not follow the other lieutenant. Thank goodness he wasn't in charge, even though he should have been. I had the remaining forty-three people follow me back up the hill and try to find enough cover to survive enemy direct fire from Fort Driant.

I had a new responsibility: the lives of my men, a glorious burden.

Litter evacuation was done by hand, one and a half miles to the river. Food and ammunition were carried back to the hill from the river through steady shelling. Casualties were high, and after four days of battling only one officer, Lt. Isaac Storey, and less than fifty men survived the ordeal. Lieutenant Storey, who took command of what was left of the company, organized the remnants and skillfully employed his troops in working their way to the high ground and keeping the enemy from destroying the bridgehead. A Silver Star award was presented to Lt. Storey for his achievements during this period, as the company firmly consolidated their positions and occupied the objective under his command.[3]

Our battalion attack was the third on the hill. It was not too long afterward that I called the battalion commander and told him we must be used somewhere, and that it was ridiculous for us to be annihilated while simply waiting. The battalion commander suggested that I reconnoiter and see if we might be placed on the top of the hill along the defense line. He said that he didn't know who was left or where they were. I did as he suggested and found that there was a gap between two other units already on the hill. This gap would require about the number of people I had left.

I was able to find and count forty-three survivors from approximately 165 of our company. I led them, without the remaining officer, back up the hill. I knew I had to find a place for them, which turned out to be a patch of woods that provided some cover. It was necessary that we hide during that day's light to avoid the Germans retaking the hill. Night came, and we divided into two groups. My half stayed among the trees. I sent a message to the acting battalion commander that we must not stay in our position. Where should I locate my remnant of about forty people? His answer was that he didn't know enough about the situation to tell me, but he asked me to reconnoiter and make a decision. I walked to the top of our hill, found an unoccupied space on our hill and three or four people who had separated from the 11th Infantry. I took about thirty of my people to set up a defense of that empty area.

I had one soldier with a 30-caliber machine gun from our weapons platoon and another from the 11th. This fortuitous arrangement repulsed five nightly attacks directed toward the formerly undefended space. Again, twenty-five or so gutsy young men saved the day and night. I was carrying only a carbine. All we had were rifles: the M1 rifle and Browning automatic rifle. Each platoon only had one bazooka.

As I got the men together (and this was a long day of trying to get situated and protect whoever we could), we received a lot of artillery fire. I thought at first it was our artillery that we had ordered, but I was wrong. It turned out the Germans in the nearby Fort Driant had observations on our positions and were listening in on my requests over the radio. When our artillery fired, it went where I wanted it to, and the Germans fired at the same time right into us. That was one of their tricks. We knew they were listening to our radio transmissions.

We suffered some more casualties that night. I was extremely emotional about that the next morning.

Our area was struck by a counterattack, which we turned back by inflicting an enormous number of German casualties. It was important to hold the line of defense on the hill. We later learned that this hill had been a practice area for the nearby German military school.

The Germans had discovered the gap between the American troops a few days before we arrived. Their counterattacks came right in that gap for almost a week. The Germans directed their nighttime counterattacks, so they thought they had the perfect way to penetrate our defense. The gap was only about 100 yards wide, but it could be defended with just a few soldiers spread out across it. The newly established bridgehead was able to hold simply because of our defense.

I had asked for air support as soon as we discovered four tanks with turrets and guns barely visible beyond a small hill. After we had a few locator shots from the 88mm weapons, a couple guys had debris wounds from trees being hit. After what seemed like years of waiting, finally, on the east side of the Moselle, two P-47 airplanes saved our necks. Two of them flew in above the hill. As they flew into our space, one of them dropped a 500-pound bomb too close to us for comfort. They circled once, then were able to see the four German tanks, circled again and dropped one more, knocking out the track of one. That crew exited in a hurry, and I could hear the engines as they cranked up and began a slow retreat. As the three remaining Panzers began to back away slowly, the successful pilot flew right above me and gave a snappy salute. I've tried several times to identify that pilot. I eventually tracked down the unit but not that day's crew. I have saluted him many times in absentia ever since.

The P-47 pilots estimated that there were 500 German bodies that surrounded us from days of relentless fighting. I thought, however, that our P-47 pilots who flew over the scene exaggerated their description of what they saw!

For four days the enemy tried probing attacks, and for the next seven days we defended this spot. I stayed awake for a total of six days and nights because I had the responsibility for those guys, and if something had happened—even if somebody had gotten scared and had run back—it would have opened up a hole in our lines.

Official Citation

For gallantry in action on 11 September 1944 in the vicinity of Arry, France. Under a relentless barrage of enemy artillery, mortar and small arms fire, the enemy forces attempted three strong counterattacks which were completely repulsed on each attempt. The enemy's repeated offensives proved costly to our forces both in officers and enlisted personnel. Lieutenant STOREY, the lone remaining officer in the company, with utter disregard for personal safety, efficiently and skillfully succeeded in organizing the remaining men in the company and aggressively led them to the battalion perimeter which had been pierced by the fierce enemy counterattack. Lieutenant STOREY, at all times completely exposed to the intense enemy fire, personally went from group to group encouraging his men and spurring them on to greater efforts. Due to the daring and courageous actions of Lieutenant STOREY, the company was reorganized and contributed greatly to the establishment of a bridgehead across the Moselle River. Lieutenant STOREY'S bravery and deep devotion to duty, his intrepidity and skillful leadership reflects great credit on himself and is in keeping with the highest traditions of the military service.[4]

Finding out in December 1944 that I had been awarded a Silver Star was really quite a surprise. When the battalion executive officer told me about the award, I said, "What for?" For one thing there were so few people left in the company after the Moselle River crossing in September that I was surprised to learn that anybody had enough details that could be used to ask for a citation. I also felt I had done what I trained to do in a commitment to defeat the enemy and care for the men in my command. It was actually my concern for the few men who were left that led me to do what turned out to be very fortuitous for the success of the bridgehead.

The battle continued. Badly needed reinforcements, including officers, joined the company. Moving to the right of Arry, the company cleared out of the wooded area and then proceeded to the outskirts of Pournoy-la-Chétive, where they received orders to relieve another company in Pournoy. The company entered the town on the afternoon of the 30th of September, and the sight of burning tanks and a field littered with mutilated bodies was proof of the ferocity of the fighting in that area. By the evening of the same day, the troops barely got into positions when the Germans made a desperate counterattack. It was stopped mainly through the efforts of Cannon Co.'s pinpoint fire that was directed on the enemy tanks and infantry, which were only a hundred yards away from the troops. Although the counterattack was broken up, the threat to recapture the town continued. Throughout the night, shrieks and eerie noises filled the air, coming from the wounded German soldiers who were hit by our artillery and cannons. The next morning revealed many bodies sprawled in grotesque positions, the result of a futile enemy attack.[5]

The next morning at dawn I found several more had been killed and wounded. Among those I found dead was the remarkable Private "Bug Eye" Brown, a kid with a sense of humor, a clown who kept us going even in the most difficult times. He actually saved us from ourselves a few times. The only time I remember actually shedding some tears in combat was as I stood by the shallow foxhole where he lay. I cannot put into words the struggle of being with a comrade around your age or a bit older and holding him as he dies. In their last breaths many of them talk to their mothers, and there was another who begged me not to let him die because he would never see his child again. These are the images and memories that are the hardest when they pass through my mind. I will always equally remember all the funny times and darn good folks and soldiers that they were.

At one point another American battalion caught up to us. We were delighted to hear that they parked their tank right near our position. After making some conversation one afternoon, there was one young guy who came over to me and asked if I knew how to pray. As we sat, I tried to explain briefly about God, faith, and how prayer "worked."

Just before dusk, he left and said he was going to sleep under his tank. He asked if I wanted to join him for protection. The next morning we found him dead from shrapnel from a nearby bomb. A brief, beautiful moment in the middle of this horrible war. A brief, beautiful moment that ended in tragedy. This is one of the many heavy memories that I carry with me to this day.

Our success was due to the fact that we were not assigned to be anywhere else. These few actions, dictated by necessity and by an intense desire to make the bridgehead succeed, made it possible to hang on, finally, to the east side of the Moselle.

For the next three days and nights the company was on the receiving of heavy enemy artillery fire from the surrounding forts and tanks. Machine guns chattered almost continuously, and along with sniper fire at night, rain and mud played havoc with the men in the foxholes. Although "C" Company received many casualties, the Germans suffered much more due to the support from our artillery units. Supplies could only be brought to the troops at night, and vehicles dared not roam the area because of enemy direct fire.[6]

Following the successful defense on Hill 386, we took refuge in the closest town to the east, Pournoy-la-Grasse, where I spent the night of my twenty-second birthday in the basement of a house in the middle of town. Our location served as the command post. We were supposed to have a radio operator with us, but we didn't have one that evening. A sound-powered telephone was the only means of communication for us. We needed to have wire connected to one of our new observation sites, so I had a runner unreel the wire. It took him about seven trips to make the connection. The last time he came in, he begged me not to send him again. Later that night, the whole house above the basement was blown away.

Daylight and hiding time made it now feasible to try again. The trudge back across a dark field and through the dark woods back to the Arry Hill represented a feeling of defeat since we had held on to the first successful capture of the hill, which had been so exciting.

On Sunday, the 24th of September, the company received orders to withdraw from the town. No sooner than they had evacuated their positions that night, the Germans were heard moving in.

During the past two weeks the fighting was violent, and the troops suffered more casualties than they did in the past two months. However, progress was being maintained and the loss of men was justified. The final mission of this war was to stop a madman's dynastic and territorial dream of a pagan totalitarian coalition that was self-admittedly the enemy of everything that our civilization stood for. The war was still in its early stages, but the enemy knew we were getting stronger. They fought frantically as we came closer to their homeland.[7]

Notes

[1] *The History of Company C, 10th Infantry U.S. Inf. Fifth Division, in the Battle of Europe*, 5.

[2] Ibid., 6.

[3] Ibid.

[4] "'Silver Star' by Isaac 'Harold' Storey," *Ninety Over Ninety*, accessed March 5, 2020, https://ninetyoverninety.com/silver-star-by-isaac-harold-storey/.

[5] *The History of Company C, 10th Infantry U.S. Inf. Fifth Division, in the Battle of Europe*, 7.

[6] Ibid.

[7] Ibid., 8.

September 16, 1944–
October 16, 1944:
Operations Against Metz
and Withdrawal

The battle-scarred veterans, what was left of them, moved to new positions overlooking the town of Maurielles. It was the old Maginot Line, and from these positions, the city of Metz could be seen on a clear day. But in between these two places was German-infested land. Action was limited to patrols in this area, but artillery and mortar fire from the enemy guns was zeroed in on the pill boxes and kept dropping rounds in the area, particularly at chow time, making it inconvenient for the troops. At Buery's Ford, where an OP (operating post) was stationed, enemy activity was consistent. On one instance, it was saved from a possible capture when Sgt. Richard Fowell, on a contact patrol between posts, spotted Germans sneaking toward the house. He climbed through a back window and warned the guards just in time to ward off the intruders, although the enemy did set foot in the house. Another OP wasn't as fortunate, and the entire post was captured by the defensive setup. Alertness was the password, as they had to contend with enemy patrols, artillery fire and the autumn rains.

After a week's occupation of this position, the company received orders to help out in another mission. There seemed to be no end to the hard and relentless fighting as the company moved into the Fort Driant area. This fort consisted of several buildings made of steel and cement constructed in defilade positions. It was on the west side of the Moselle River and proved to be the hardest fort to capture—the siege lasting till after the fall of Metz. It was practically impossible to make a direct assault on the fort because of the features of the main fort. Many guns, including long range artillery pieces on movable bases, gave the enemy enough fire to keep the advancing troops at a safe distance. Another feature of Fort Driant was the fact that all buildings were connected through subterranean passages. American artillery and 155s only nicked the mighty structure, and the troops were too close to have aerial bombs dropped on it.

Capture of the southern wing was not too much trouble for German General Warnock's Task Force, but as the battle progressed, it was found that the troops were losing heavily in the face of small rains. The company moved into the Port area loaded down with TNT and explosive charges. On the night of October 9, and early the next morning, they were immediately initiated by the Fort's guns. Above the ground, the troops were shelled almost continuously and communications were disrupted many times. Several times PFC Warren Mullens braved enemy barrages to keep the communication lines intact between the platoons and the CP, as the radios were useless in that setup. Shelling was too intense. Even casualties were difficult to remove to safety, and it wasn't unusual for the troops to lie alongside a dead comrade for three days. Supply was another problem. Tanks were used, and only at night did they move into a defilade position several hundred yards from the CP and drop off supplies. From there the supplies were hand carried over shell-ridden ground to the CP then to the platoons and casualties resulted from this short but important mission.

The building which housed the CP was a German target, and one morning a German tank crept up to within 50 feet of the building and blasted the walls with direct fire. Bazooka fire chased the tank away but not until it shot a hole in the wall. German soldiers armed with TNT were killed while charging the CP with the tanks. They were attempting to destroy that part of the building for future attacks. The battlefield was also marked with several American tanks afire from German hits.

Inside the underground tunnels also raged a futile battle. Plans to enter the other building by these passages were found impossible to execute as steel doors had to be penetrated by blasting with TNT. Working also with the company were the Engineers. They had the job of clearing obstacles for the underground fighters, but the explosions and concussions only harassed the troops and little damage was done to the steel doors. Although several hundred yards had been gained in these tunnels, it was given up because the process was slow. After four days of blistering warfare, the company left the fort area on October 12 under the cover of darkness and steady rain. The next day the company went back across the Moselle to Onville for a day's rest.

On the following day they were back on the positions overlooking Mauri-elles, until they were relieved by the 95th Division on the 21st of October.[1]

Training Period

For the next ten days the company went back to Ville-au-Montois, a small French town, and had a strenuous training period, stressing the attack of pillboxes and getting acquainted with new material. Those ten days weren't intended for a rest period, but it was a mental and physical relaxation because it marked the first time since starting the drive in Normandy that the company enjoyed any length of time in the rear echelon area. Recreation for the troops was provided by movies and a sports program. On November 1, the company headed for the front again and went back into the muddy foxholes.[2]

Note

[1] *The History of Company C, 10th Infantry U.S. Inf. Fifth Division, in the Battle of Europe*, 9.
[2] Ibid, 10.

November 9, 1944:
The Return to Metz

Then came General Patton's all-out offensive which led to the fall of Metz. This prize city was the gateway to the Saar Basin. Its railways and fine roads made it a modern commercial city, although the population didn't exceed 60,000 even in peacetime. The city of Metz was always an objective of European conquerors and was the world's most fortified with approximately 22 forts surrounding the area. The attacking forces had to battle inclement weather, floods and stiff resistance but entered the city by direct assault-the first time since Attila the Hun accomplished it some 500 years ago. And the troops of "C" Company were one of the first units to enter the bastion city.

Little enemy resistance was encountered by the company during the early days of November as they moved through Mardigay, Lorry, Pagny-lès-Goin and Silly-en-saulnois. Near Chesney the company met the enemy and a stiff battle ensued. Most of the troops were pinned down from machine gun and mortar fire and only when Lt. Isaac Storey directed artillery fire on the German positions were the troops able to maneuver into new positions. The German ambush caught the company in an open field and while Sgt. George E. Davis was directing his platoon in giving coverage fire to the company, he was killed by enemy machine gun fire as he went to the aid of a wounded comrade. By night the enemy was dispersed and the company reorganized again, moving toward the fort next morning. This fort was large and well concealed in a forest and was perched on a hillside. The first attack on the fort, using two tanks as support, was stopped when a German anti-tank shell knocked the lead tank out. But the next day the troops infiltrated to within fifty yards of the fort and as they were about to make a final assault, the Germans put out a white flag, and the entire garrison surrendered on the morning of November 17.

Reaching the outskirts of Metz the next evening, the company stopped momentarily in a patch of woods waiting for further orders. Hastily and emotionally word was received that they'd be fighting in the streets of Metz by morning. And it was just that way, to everyone's surprise. There seemed to be a mental tension as the troops took off for the city because they heard too much of the city that schooled German officer candidates. Dropping all excess weight and loading down with extra ammunition and grenades, besides the inevitable K Ration, the troops moved out toward Metz. At 2,000 hours the advance was halted as enemy fire from a nearby fort blocked the route which was to be used. But two hours later the company was on its way, the plans being changed. Quietly as a church mouse, the troops moved 2,000 yards through open countryside and just about midnight approached a few houses at the city limits. But the enemy spotted the troops and began throwing 20 and 30mm shells in the area, coming from the direction in which they were to move. But a quick change in plans, again by Lt. Isaac Storey and the company officers, was responsible for the successful entering of the city.[1]

I have not found any other accounts that tell about our entry into Metz from the south. It wasn't an official operation trip. It just was the only thing I could figure out to try, even though I was scared and fearful that I may be leading my guys into a really bad situation.

There was an awful lot of rainfall during the time between the establishment of the Moselle bridgehead at Arnaville and the final approach and encirclement of Metz. The "Metz Mud" severely hampered movement on foot and by any kind of vehicle.

We had been successful in getting to the edge of the Rue Strasbourg on the east of the city during the black pre-midnight in mid-November. Our orders were to get to this street quietly, bypassing Fort Queuleu, and to follow it into the city to try to intercept German troops as they used this escape route. By now the encirclement of Metz, which has been accomplished in conjunction with the 95th Infantry Division on the north side, was nearly complete.

I gathered my company among three small houses and explained what we were to do. Then, to use a rather common description of a situation, "all hell broke loose" as we set out toward the city. The enemy had moved some troops, along with at least one anti-aircraft gun (likely 20mm) into position directly on our proposed route. We took cover again in the three houses, and I got on the radio to contact our battalion command post. They offered the choice of returning to our position near them or staying in the houses. I explained that we did not have enough time left to get back to the area of our departure under darkness and that we would be too exposed to stay where we were when daylight came. Captain Bob Todd, battalion S-3, said, "What the hell are you going to do then?" I requested permission to ask for volunteers to follow me single file across a sugar beet field toward the edge of the city while it was still dark. This route was probably forty degrees from the originally prescribed one. I had not seen any fire from that particular area. I was told it was crazy, but permission granted. I explained to the men what I was going to do and ordered one medic to stay in one of the houses with two wounded patients. As I stumbled along, I actually couldn't see how many were following as I started across the field, trying to trudge quietly in the deep mud among huge half-exposed beets.

By the time we had traveled about 200 yards, dawn began to break, and I could see that most, if not all, of my people were in a close single-file line behind me. I found out later that every man except the wounded and the medic had followed. My throat really tightened as I knew that they were as aware of the danger as I was. We were all able to be out of the field as it became light enough for us to realize that we were among the backyards of some nice-looking houses. An unsolved mystery is the inaction of a German sentry whom we passed only a few yards away. He had a rifle on his shoulder but turned away after he saw us. I think it was light enough for him to see that we were Americans, but he sounded no alarm—likely out of fear for himself as he realized he was outnumbered.

It was daylight as we came into a fairly wide street and began to pick up a few surprised enemy soldiers as we walked in columns on each side of the street in the direction of the center of the city. The street, we soon found, was Rue Strasbourg, some segment of which was our ordered objective! Since the street led directly to the east and since they had seen no other Americans, they felt they had at least a couple days or more to evacuate. Our intelligence had not informed me of their near encirclement. We later found there had been several thousand German troops still in the city.

Bypassing the German sentry walking post only fifty yards away, the troops stole their way to the city proper, and at dawn the company was slowly moving down the streets of Metz, rifles cocked and the mental tension overcome. No casualties were suffered as the company routed out the bewildered Germans from their billets and guard posts. Even the civilians were

surprised to see the American soldiers in their city and danced with joy
because they were to be free again. A command car with a German colonel
passed the entire column before realizing they were American troops. When
stopped by Sgt. August Reinhardt, he asked his captor, "When do the Ameri-
cans sleep?" Further in the city a large hospital, including the major and his
entire staff, was taken, and of the wounded patients, six were Americans
who had been captured by the Germans only a few days before.[2]

More enemy soldiers, including a colonel in a new command car,
appeared as we moved along, and most of them were actually glad to
surrender. It helped that they thought we were there in much greater
numbers. I finally lagged back with my radio man and, for the first
time since the "volunteer" conversation, tried to contact somebody in
the battalion Command Post. No luck. Then one of my people came
hurrying up to me and said that a man at the hospital gate wanted to
see the officer in charge. When I got there, a big German civilian in
good English said the commandant would be there shortly to surrender
the hospital. As we waited, we heard an artillery shell approaching, and
this big German pushed me against a brick wall on one side of the gate
and actually covered my body with his. Most of the men in the street
simply did not take cover as it was quickly obvious the shell would not
fall very close.

Quickly recovering from my surprise, I saw a colonel approaching.
He formally surrendered the hospital with a salute and a click of his
heels as he handed me a very small 9mm pistol. He then said "Now we
work for you" and went on to say he had several American prisoners as
patients and he hoped I would come back soon to see them, which I did
later in the day. I gave the very thirsty American patients a sip from my
canteen and learned the hospital had been without drinking water for
several days. They did, however, have cheap wine! They had also been
without plaster of Paris and splints and were using concrete for leg and
body casts! The German colonel had invited me to have dinner with
him in his private dining room. I accepted his offer and took my runner,
a reluctant Warren Mullins, with me. Both of us enjoyed a hot meal that
wasn't very tasty.

During the first day we captured about 400 Germans and herded
them into a walled courtyard. Close by we took defensive positions in

apartment buildings to wait out the arrival of other Americans and to capture all who came our way in the effort to escape to the east. Finally, I went to about the fifth floor of the building with a SCR 300 radio to try to contact our battalion headquarters. The same "Bob Todd" quickly came on and asked, "Where in the #@!$ hell have you been? We thought all of you were dead!" I replied that we'd been busy and asked if they would send people to take charge of a few hundred prisoners. To poke good fun, I even reminded him of the no cussing rules of military radio communications. It was certain Metz would fall in a couple days.

Meanwhile, several newsmen braved the uncertainty of the situation and anxiously interviewed me and several of my troops. I donated to them the German staff car and advised the happy recipients to get another kind of paint on it quickly. Transportation for them had been quite difficult as they sweated the fall of the city. Among these reporters was Lewis Hawkins, an Associated Press newsman who had been stationed in Atlanta. I have ever since been indebted to him for using my name as he reported the capture of Metz, partly because of the leadership of a "Georgia boy" named Isaac H. Storey. The story was carried in the *Atlanta Constitution* and several other papers around the state the next day. My parents were delighted to learn that at least in the last twenty-four hours I had been alive. This was, by weeks, the freshest news they had of my activities.

It was pouring down rain in Metz when the company was preparing to eat a delicious Thanksgiving Day dinner. But a sudden change in orders interrupted the affair, and a rain-soaked outfit moved to Plappeville on the outskirts of Metz to relieve another unit. This fort, like most other forts, was built on the side of a mountain and had a moat around it, and a drawbridge was the only means of getting to it. Activity amounted to almost nothing except to keep a siege of the fort. On November 27 the company was relieved, but before going back, the troops were fed an enormous dinner put out by Sgt. Jim Clegg and his culinary artists—a meal that probably never will be surpassed in Army history for a frontline outfit. It was Thanksgiving as far as chow was concerned.

After billeting in a former German OCS building for several days at Metz-Ost, the company was on the move again. It was the beginning of a new campaign, but a short one. Leaving Bisten-en-Lorraine, the company

began a seven-day woods-clearing, starting near Diesen, France, and cross-
ing the German border into Ludwiler, Germany. Resistance was still active,
and the troops advanced slowly, mostly due to the skirmishes and rear guard
opposition. But they were able to take prisoners as they went along. Moving
east of Creutwald, the troops gained 1,200 yards and crossed the German
border for the first time during this war, with Sgt. August Reinhards. In this
area of woods, the company was operating in conjunction with the famous
5th Rangers in pocketing a German unit. A German squad that refused to
give up when trapped in a coal mine had to be annihilated before the troops
could occupy the buildings. The severe fighting continued the next day when
the company, supported by four tanks, cleared a large area of woods and a
town, capturing an important crossroads and inflicting heavy casualties on
the enemy. The company casualties were moderate, considering the resistance
and terrain obstacles to overcome.

The company entered the town of Ludwiler a few days later, but the
enemy was unorganized and offered little fighting to the hardened, grimy
troops. The next twelve days were fairly inactive, so the company enjoyed a
period of relaxation. But on December 19 an alert order was issued concern-
ing a German counterattack. That turned out to be the Battle of the Bulge.[3]

Notes

[1] *The History of Company C, 10th Infantry U.S. Inf. Fifth Division, in the Battle of Europe*, 10–12.

[2] Ibid., 9.

[3] Ibid., 13–15.

The Battle of the Bulge

Having finally entered and cleared out Metz about November 18, we started toward a destination we passionately dreaded—the German border and the Siegfried line. Snow was already falling, an enemy in itself, because it made the German observation of our movements easier, and it was difficult to find a place warm enough to allow us some sleep. The big thing was that we knew the Germans would defend their border more vigorously than they had many of the French places during late summer. (I think they thought their own border just couldn't be breached).

On December 19 battalion and regimental senior officers came to forward positions to find those of us who were company commanders. They informed us personally that German Panzer divisions had been amassed to attack our front. Of course, we were all surprised to know they had such capability—and honestly we hoped the strike would be to the east!

The breakthrough across the German border, which seemed suddenly to have generated a blinding speed, enveloped the German people and army in amazement, like a shot in the arm. What a tremendous opportunity to a defeat-weary German people; what a fatal blunder if the effort failed. To the Americans it was a fanatically mad drive, costing the Germans twice as many men and five times the material as the Allies. Its reasons are still debated, and even military strategists fail to see the object of the Ardennes push—especially so late in the game. But well-trained, seasoned troops were needed to halt this advance, and the 5th Division was called to assist on the southern flank. After making the 100-mile trip from Ludwilder, Germany, the troops detrucked four miles from the city of Luxembourg and early next morning began to hunt down the foe.

For the next six days the company moved into the Luxembourg mountains, treading their way through snow and cold weather, meeting strong enemy resistance. This drive, which was part of the southern flank, drove the enemy back and kept the Nazi threat from the city of Luxembourg, which was part of their objective in the Ardennes counteroffensive. On December 20 "C" Company started hunting down German paratroopers and ground forces about four miles northeast of Luxembourg City. They moved cautiously as they approached the town of Bech, fighting for high ground.

Christmas Eve found the company three miles northeast of Bech, atop a high mountain overlooking the quiet, moonlit, snow-covered valley that led to Echternach. It was a perfect setting for Christmas, but nobody had much time to think about it. The men were busy setting up a defense for the night. Early the next morning the drive continued, and it was here that the offensive reached its climax. A German battalion was destined to hold until the end. After a pitched battle, twenty-seven prisoners were captured, the remainder of the battalion killed, and only a few escaped. A wounded German captain admitted his unit was wiped out. American artillery, dropping close to the lines, helped considerably in routing the defenders. Christmas night was spent in foxholes in zero-degree temperatures. On December 26 "C" Company moved rapidly, picking up sixteen remaining prisoners and gaining the objective at 1,300 hours. From this high terrain, which was one mile south of Echternach, the dragon's teeth of the Siegfried line, which later was assaulted in another point, could be seen. After being relieved, the company moved back to Kodenbour in Luxembourg, where they ate their Christmas dinner.[1]

On Christmas Eve, the eighth day of these conditions, the skies became blue, and I stood by a snow-laden fir tree and thanked God I could hear and eventually see a steady line of planes above! (Patton claimed this was an answer to his own prayers; which makes me wonder how God filters a profane prayer.) Our planes kept coming the next few days and apparently did enough damage to effectively turn the tide, allowing us time to find cover for the night. A few of us crawled into part of a small barn and found soft hay there. We stretched out about midnight, and immediately a stranger stuck his head inside and asked for me. He had a few packages for our company, and one was for me—a box of cookie crumbs sent weeks before by Merle Croucher, the wife of a fellow officer friend from Indianapolis. The crumbs lasted about four minutes as I recall.

Christmas Day brought beautiful weather and an idyllic setting with snow on every branch of fir trees, ten- to fifteen-feet tall, planted in rows. In the valley sat many mostly damaged and abandoned bed and breakfast houses and small inns. Many of the men were very weary and deeply depressed. I tried to offer some encouragement for these men as we approached the forward slope of the mountain. The top of the mountain provided good observation of the approach to the Sauer River.

As I stood at the edge of a little road waiting for the rest of my folks to get oriented and catch up, Private First Class Castle approached me. He was a replacement medic who had endeared himself to all of us. He always wanted to do anything he could—cheerfully—including trudging back a mile or so to bring five-gallon cans of water whenever we got a message that water was available. This time he asked my permission to go back to where he had seen two wounded Germans, an officer and enlisted man, and try to "fix up" their wounds. At first I told him I'd rather he not go alone, that he should not separate from the group and go alone. He indicated the direction, said it wasn't far, and that he would be back in a hurry. I was impressed with the great compassion of this young kid and felt it an appropriate act for Christmastime anywhere. His commitment was to people, not just friends or allies.

As mid-darkness started to fall, one of my platoon leaders found me and asked about Castle. I told him what had transpired and said I thought I could find him. After searching down a couple rows, I did indeed find him. His hand was under the wounded arm of one of the two still-alive Germans. Castle was dead from a bullet through his helmet. My emotions nearly tore me apart! Anger raged through me like never before. It was expected for me to shoot the squirming and begging German men laying on the ground. I cocked and raised my carbine and pointed it at the captain.

Immediately, images of my family ran through my head. Today was Christmas Day. Somehow I thought that if I did survive, I would never want to remember that I had killed two helpless people on Christmas. I would not want my family to know I had done such a thing. It was really mostly selfish with some compassion thrown in. I also knew this would not be a fitting tribute to the short and beautiful life Castle had lived. I didn't pull the trigger.

I did not know where Castle was from and have never been able to find his family since. Years after the war, I did find his serial number. My request to search for military records has been answered but has never been successful. It's very difficult for non-family members to get information on soldiers through Army records—rightly so. We never discovered who had killed Castle, possibly somebody hiding nearby even as I stood there beside his body and the terrified Germans. We found out later that the Germans were evacuated and were safe in a hospital. I am forever glad I didn't yield to my temptation to take their lives.

After a short break the company then moved to a new area, where they went into a defensive position, setting up outposts. The new positions were taken up at Reisdorf, Luxembourg, on January 1. After a short stay there, the company then moved about a mile and relieved "I" Company of the 10th at Ermadorf, posting guards and running contact patrols. This position overlooked the German defenses across the Sauer River, and sporadic sniper fire harassed the company.

Being relieved after six days in Ermsdorf, the company moved into another defensive setup near the town of Clairefontaine. This also was a period of inactivity aside from the outposting along the Sauer River. However, our outposts did fire artillery on enemy targets across the river, and patrols were active along the river. Early the morning January 19 "C" Company started on another offensive. Snow and cold prevailed with white camouflage suits as the dress. Just as they approached the river, the company had to dodge rockets and artillery for 200 yards before crossing on a footbridge and taking cover in Gilsdorf, about a half mile from Diekirch on the other side of the Sauer. That same night the company climbed the steep, high hill in the face of a heavy downpour of rain and dug in. The next day positions were advanced, and the company set up on the top of this high hill where activity was limited to heavy artillery. The only excitement came when a German rocket hit a large barn, setting it afire. All the troops inside escaped the inferno, but some equipment was lost. From here the troops moved forward and entered Bastendord and after a night's rest rode trucks to a new position.[2]

That very night the Germans launched an attack that would result in the involvement of a total of 600,000 troops, the largest single battle in history. We were just inside the German border in the Saar Valley, and during the night we got orders to climb on any vehicle heading north.

It was one of Patton's miracles that we arrived in the middle of Luxembourg not long after dawn, 100 miles away, slipping and sliding in deeper and deeper snow. Rumors were rampant as we were told that Germans had filtered into our ranks in American uniforms, that a lot of our weapons had been captured, and that many atrocities were being committed.

The next few days, cloudy and bitterly cold, were a nightmare of danger in one of the most beautiful places in the world. Casualties from artillery, tanks firing through the trees, and rifle fire, bup gums, and trench foot kept depleting our ranks as we were trying to push back that part of the "Bulge."

It was hard to decide which was the #1 enemy—Germans or the snowy, cloudy weather.

At 0730 hours on January 22, the company began what turned out to be a disastrous engagement. Moving carefully up the snow-covered valley, the company reached the high ground on the same afternoon amid mortar and artillery fire. Here they entrenched themselves in a patch of woods overlooking the enemy held territory. But German observation was good on that sunny day and the troops were subject to heavy and accurate artillery barrages. On this hill the company suffered casualties and among those wounded were Lt. Storey, commanding officer, who refused to leave.3

While somebody searched for Lt. Robert Dunn, the Company 2nd in command, two aid men had arrived in a Jeep to take Storey to an aid station on the edge of Diekirch. They got him across deep snow along a hard-to-see woods track and were finally able to get him to an aid station in a small church at the edge of Diekirch.[4]

By now we thought the war or winter would never end; troops dwindled to weakened strengths. But on January 22 (which turned out to be the official last day of the Bulge battle) it was over for me. Two artillery men had come over to talk to me after we spotted enemy movement on the next hill. I was standing between these two men when a mortar shell hit a tree limb about eighteen inches from my head.

The two men on either side of me were killed instantly. I looked down at them and saw their eyes still staring at me as they had seconds before. My face felt numb, and I couldn't hear anything. We all were wearing hooded white canvas jackets with white trousers. I didn't realize what had happened until blood, delayed by the bitter cold, began dripping from my neck down onto the white clothing.

It was shrapnel. The largest piece was between my windpipe and my jugular vein. I had four little pieces in my back, one in my arm, and one in my leg. Another piece left a large hole straight through my canteen.

I was crouched down trying to see how badly our platoon leader had been wounded in the face. He would not let me look at his face as he held it and blood poured through his fingers.

Lieutenant Robert Dunn immediately replaced me as company commander.

Soon, two people were grabbing at my collar to pull me up to give me the prescribed sulfa tablets. They then began sort of dragging me toward a small track in the snow. Shortly after, a Jeep came, and I was helped into a seat as we proceeded down a steep hill. The Jeep slid off the little road and got stuck in the snow. It was about to get dark, and it wasn't long until they got enough people to push and pull and get us on the way down the hill to an aid station at the little Catholic church in Diekirch.

Somebody gave me a shot that I'm sure was pain medication. A young man looked at the bandage and gingerly aided my shoulder. He moved on to a couple of shivering people. Soon, I was loaded into an ambulance. I marveled at the warmth in the vehicle!

After a warm and relatively painless ambulance trip, we were rolled into a large room filled with people, all very quiet waiting for one of the people moving between patients asking questions. As I lay there with my eyes closed thinking about the guys I had just left, I became aware that somebody who was standing by me smelled wonderful—and I said so. A very attractive young nurse thanked me and said she needed to help me get undressed to get an X-ray.

Next was a large room where several surgical operations were going on. There were about seventeen surgeries that I was put in line for. I remember the man ahead of me had his legs amputated. I was wheeled into a slot and suddenly surrounded by about six serious but pleasant people who felt I needed to be told all they knew about my situation. One man said I'd be getting sodium pentathol and that I'd occasionally be aware that they were working with a wound in my neck, which, if it became infected that close to the brain, would be very dangerous. He asked, "Are you afraid to die?" I said no, and he asked why the hell my heartbeat was so rapid. I said, "I am not afraid to die, but I certainly don't want to!"

There was one doctor who was assigned to just watch my face and give me more medication if I were to wake up. I did indeed wake up three times during that surgery. The piece of shrapnel in my neck was so close that they were afraid to use the sharp medical instruments. The surgeon had to open up the wound to use his fingers to probe and remove the shrapnel. The recovery immediately after the surgery was very painful as I could not move my neck or sit up for food or drink.

I was taken from there to Luxembourg City to a convent being used as a hospital, where I had surgery and spent several days. Shortly after, I was informed that we would be boarding a train for Paris. We were to travel in a box car with litters stacked three to a side, a wood stove for heat, and one nurse to look after us. Before getting on the box car, the hospital in Luxembourg had taken me out of my pajamas. They laid us on the litters only covered by bandages and a very scratchy German blanket. I bet none of my readers have traveled to Paris naked!

Before boarding the train, we were placed in holding tents on the ground, where the wind whipped under the tent flaps while the train was being placed for loading. This was the first operating train I had seen because the retreating Germans had destroyed most of the rail lines as they could to impede our movement.

On arrival in Paris we were moved from transport to large rooms at the American Hospital for further surgeries before I was sent to England. I saw a lot of ceilings and sky only because up to now I dared not turn my head because of the wound in my neck. German prisoners with noisy hobnail boots lifted our stretchers to their shoulders and typically walked in step. It wasn't a fun sound.

A train then took us to Le Havre for loading on a hospital ship, then to Southampton, then to 119th General Hospital at Blandford Forum near Salisbury.

I had a remarkable recovery during the next three months in the surgical wing of the 119th General Hospital. All grades of officers were in the same ward; likewise, enlisted men of various ranks were together.

There were frequent trips for ambulatory patients via buses to neighboring towns. One of our nurses asked me one day if I liked music. I said it would be great to hear a fine orchestra. "Then we'll go to Bournemouth next Sunday," she replied. We ate a snack at the Red Cross club, and I suggested we return to the hospital because I just didn't want to be seen limping. Nor did I want to show off a scar that was so obvious. She convinced me to try the earlier shows of the symphony. And so we went! Of course it was a magnificent concert—with an organist, about eighty years old, who at times seemed to lift the roof from the walls. I attended several more times and persuaded several different people to go with me.

As I finished recovering at the hospital, I had some communication with a cousin who was a medic at a hospital not far from Salisbury. I didn't know where the hospital was, but I had to get somebody to find out and tell him I was only a few miles away. When he did have the chance to come see me, he stood about sixty feet away for a while before he approached the bed. He was happy to find out I had all my arms and legs.

He helped me get in touch with my parents. I could not remember the last time I had talked to them. I told them where my wounds were and that I was deaf in my right ear for a while.

My cousin told me I should get a photograph when I fully recovered. I borrowed some uniform and infantry insignia and went to a professional photographer in Salisbury and had a picture made that I sent back to my family. That's really the only picture I have with me in my uniform.

It was amusing to reconnect with some of the men I had left later after the war. One said he had heard that a German bayonet had gone right through my neck and I had survived. Another thought I had survived a bullet through the neck. Although neither was right, it was amusing to hear that speculation.

Notes

[1] *The History of Company C, 10th Infantry U.S. Inf. Fifth Division, in the Battle of Europe,* 13–15.

[2] Ibid., 17.

[3] Ibid., 17–18.

[4] Ibid., 18.

Warton Trade School

The Warton American Technical School, established in Freckleton, England, right off the Irish Sea, was my last overseas assignment. It turned out to be a great experience, although it would delay my getting home for many months. I am very thankful to have been a part of this assignment at the end of WWII.

After fully recovering from my wounds, a colonel I knew found me in the hospital area in southern England before I was released, and he said, "Storey, I've got orders for us to go to northern England to get a project started that the Army has got an idea about." This was not really a problem for me because I did not have any specific assignment at the moment. About two days had passed before I met up with the colonel again, and we took his Jeep to head north. We rode for a few hours from Salisbury, England, to a place on the Irish Seas known as Freckleton. It is a beautiful, famous place.

We found our assignment was to establish a technical school for GIs. There were thousands of soldiers still stationed in Europe waiting for orders to go home. All were obviously anxious, so the idea was to allow them to go to eight weeks of tech school in various programs. We had a site in Freckleton that had been used as a B-17 bomber repair station, and had also served as an old British school. On August 24, 1944, an American B-24 liberator crashed into the school, three houses, and a local business. On the day of this disaster, a bad storm came in shortly after two B-24s took off. They were ordered to return to base. One plane landed safely, but the other one was brought down by the storm. I later learned that over sixty people had been killed during this disaster, most of whom were children. The local business that was destroyed was called the "Sad Shack" by many of the guys who hung out at the popular bar.

It was very sad to know of the loss of life from this tragic accident. Airmen raised money, and shortly afterward a memorial garden and children's playground were opened. I remember the talks of a better memorial, and finally, in 1977, a memorial hall was opened. I relived this disaster through the other guys stationed there, and I see it as a story that should be shared. I was not there during the disaster but arrived later to help with rebuilding the school. We began our work exactly after we were told how to accomplish our task. We were promised men who were in the same situation as we were. These would-be men were awaiting one more assignment before getting orders to come home. Our goal was to get 4,000 students through the technical school in one term. One term lasted a total of eight weeks. We were expected to have graduated two terms of students from August to December.

There were classes offered in almost any field, such as art, business, industry, etc. They had classes for painting, operation of cranes, automotive repair, and many other mostly technical studies. This was a challenge we liked, because we were promised that the people who would help us were the instructors who would lead the classes. The instructors, who all came from the United States, were very good leaders in their fields.

We had a nice officers' mess, barracks for enlisted men, and adequate space for junior and senior officers. Since we were lieutenants, we never had much of a choice in quarters, but this time we were given a really nice space. However, we were told that if the higher brass came along, we may have to give up our space. As you can imagine, the higher officers did show up, so we had to pack our stuff and move into lesser quarters. At my suggestion, a few of the guys with whom I had been in the hospital moved into an enlisted barracks. There were about seven or eight of us, and we could fix up our space the way we wanted it. The officers' mess was still close by, and convenient. This turned out to be an ideal situation.

The fun included the instruction and the leadership of the civilians who had come. GE, Westinghouse, and other major U.S. companies sent people. We even had special uniforms for the civilian instructors to wear during their time with us. Coming up with all the materials and equipment for our school would prove to be difficult work. We had hoped to open in August, and I believe we did right at the end of the month, though there was a lot to do to make that deadline. We had to borrow beds from Oxford University, which was the closest of the two major universities.

Being on orders in Freckleton was also a great time for reflection and socializing. A lot of the guys who were working to get this school going would become really good friends before it was over. It turned out to be a wonderful experience, one I've called the ideal PTSD experience. I had time to ease up and deal with the experiences of the war before going home. I also had other men who went through many similar things, so we could talk about this stuff with like-minded new veterans.

The living was good, the pay okay. We had some good civilian help, and I even had a female secretary who was very attractive. Everybody there thought I had picked her out because I had gotten there early, but that was not the case. I worked my tail off trying to be the person who procured the stuff we needed. I turned out to be a twenty-three-year-old gopher because I had been there the longest, and everybody asked me every question. This kind of led me to having some sort of authority. I even met some captains and lieutenant colonels who would come to ask me what I thought about something. We had to make satisfactory accommodations with the general and his so-called "lady in waiting," who was an attractive English lady!

I have thought many times how great was the Freckleton experience, for it prepared me to come home. They talked about throwing a big birthday party for me around the time we opened the school. Well, they did throw a party, and it was quite a celebration. It was one I still remember very well! That was definitely an ideal way to spend some time in the military!

Journey to America

World War II ended with the unconditional surrender of Germany in May 1945, but both May 8 and May 9 are celebrated as Victory in Europe Day, or V-E Day. This double celebration occurs because the Germans surrendered to the Western Allies, including Britain and the United States on May 8, and a separate surrender took place on May 9 in Russia. The war with Japan ended when the United States dropped atomic bombs on Hiroshima and Nagasaki on August 6 and 9 respectively. The date of the Japanese surrender is known as Victory Over Japan Day, or V-J Day.

I found out I would go home during Christmas of 1945. I was to return to the United States on the U.S.S. Lake Champlain, a new aircraft carrier that had been assigned to bring us home.

I arrived in the wee hours of Christmas Eve at Fort Gordon in Augusta, Georgia. My parents had come to wait, not knowing when our troop train would get there from Camp Kilmer in New Jersey. It took a really long time getting to Augusta. We had to make unscheduled stops for toilet facilities and to have cold sandwiches and drinking water delivered to us, because the toilets and water fountains on the entire train were frozen during the whole trip from Camp Kilmer.

After a few hours of details at Fort Gordon, my parents picked me up in a glorious reunion, and we left for a long-awaited trip to Crystal Springs in Floyd County, Georgia. As we let out a friend in Atlanta, we discovered that the rain that had started was now freezing. Dreading the trip driving after dark, we were driving very carefully. As we passed up a hill near Kennesaw, we realized that an oncoming car was headed straight at us! The driver, surprised by the ice, hit his brakes and traveled right into our car head-on. Our car was totaled; my mother had a cut on her knee. My forehead broke the windshield, and my dad had a painful rib fracture.

While I stayed to dispose of the car and to find a way home, a Greyhound bus driver directly behind us asked if he could take my parents home to Rome, Georgia. I was able to talk the wrecker driver, who had tire chains, into bringing me to McCall Hospital to catch up with my parents. By the time I arrived at McCall hospital it was 2:00 AM. Finally, a neighbor arrived to take us to Crystal Springs.

A Man of Peace

They say that war is the greatest thing to happen to every generation so we can look back and learn from history's mistakes. One of the main things I always carry with me is the memory of the men and brothers who were killed by my side overseas. After I took over as company commander, I felt responsible for the lives of the men under me. We never used the term "survivor's guilt" back then, but shortly after the war, I did catch myself wishing I had known more about what was going on with each person who served with me. Especially if there was a casualty under my command, I think about ways that things could have turned out differently. I have lived the last seventy-five years reminding myself that fighting in this war was our responsibility, and our duty. We tried our hardest.

After the war, I traveled to several different states and visited the parents and families of many dear friends that were killed. I found that many soldiers, now veterans, and families who lost their sons, husbands, brothers, and fathers all asked the same question: "Where do we go from here?" Everyone has different answers to this question. In the last seventy-five years, I have found mine: Whoever is leading us from here, we have to trust. After the war, if God gave me a vision as to what was next, if he immediately told me what I was supposed to do, then I would have never had any reason to use my faith. This faith has led me to a wonderful life full of family, friendships, and countless experiences. I have also found that it is my responsibility to care for and remember the lives of everyone who has entered my life, living and dead.

Having witnesses suffering, war, hardship, death, and witnessing the innocent struggle firsthand, I have dedicated my life to always fight for peace.

What is one thing I want to be remembered for? Well, seventy-five years after these terrible times, they call us heroes. I still see myself back then as a twenty-two-year-old Georgia boy who was just doing my part.

Even if I was called to be a schoolteacher or a ditch digger, I would have done my part and strived to do the right thing. But I was called to be a soldier, so this is my story.

Afterword

Reflections on 70 Years of Marriage:
A Dialogue

"People are unique, one of a kind, and Harold is no exception! He can be described in many ways and in particular terms."—Rena Storey

Rena Storey:

Harold and I met in 1946, the year of my graduation from Hollins College in Roanoke, Virginia. He had returned from Europe on Christmas Day, 1945. Here is his version of our meeting: We were part of a group invited to a dinner party in Atlanta to celebrate the twenty-first birthday of a mutual friend. We gathered at a home in Rome before leaving for Atlanta. Several of us were there when Harold came in. According to Harold, I was introduced, said "hello," and went on talking to the person next to me. I do remember meeting him! His designated date happened to be spending the night with me, and he brought her to my house after the party. On September 27, 1950, his date that earlier night was my matron of honor at our wedding at First United Methodist Church of Rome. When we married, Harold was twenty-eight, and I was twenty-four.

Harold Storey:

Recently we have been asked how the background of a boy from the country meshed with that of a girl from town. In retrospect we can thank our parents for their attitudes. Each accepted the other's family for who they were without emphasis on differences. My mother was the best mother and mother-in-law anyone could have imagined. She was caring and supportive of Rena throughout her life. I know she was the same to my brother's wife. It was a privilege for anyone to know "Teddy," as she was called, and all loved her.

Rena Storey:

Just as Harold's outlook on life was changed by his World War II experiences, mine was transformed by my adoption in infancy by my parents. God gave them the desire to raise a child as their very own, and they gave me life. I have always felt grateful and special. Special, not in the sense of being superior, but in the knowledge of being wanted and chosen. It is a good feeling. Much later when our son Hal and daughter-in-law Terry asked my thoughts about their adopting a child, I could speak with experience and gratitude. As a result, we gained a wonderful little grandson, Blaine Christian Storey.

Harold Storey:

Ever since my childhood in the country where many came to our home seeking food, I have been concerned about the people who do not have enough to eat. My experiences in Europe made me even more aware and concerned.

Our community kitchen, called Koinonia, is a multichurch project hosted first at East Rome United Methodist church and later by our church, First Baptist Church of Rome, to feed the hungry people in our neighborhood. I should tell you how Rena came to be involved. At the time, Rena was a volunteer at Hospitality House for abused women. The director realized there was a need for a soup kitchen in the area. Rena knew she was to be part of its beginning, remembering that when she was a young girl during the Depression, her mother fed many people who came asking for food. Later she was asked to take on the job of coordinator. Seeing the dedication of our volunteers and the appreciation of the community inspired her to serve in this capacity for twenty-four years. We worked together as I proudly gave her both mental and physical support. Today we have a community kitchen located in its own building. We can no longer volunteer, but Rena's past involvement and dedication is an experience we both treasure.

Rena Storey:

Just as Harold and I have our humanity in common with those in need of a free meal, we can learn from those of different cultures. Our travels began inadvertently when we encouraged my mother in a business decision. My father's untimely death at age fifty-five when I was ten caused my mother to learn to manage income, pay household expenses, etc., without any experience. When she decided to accept an offer from someone to purchase property she owned, as we had advised, she gave us a reward, funds for a month-long trip to Europe. She knew Harold wanted very much to go back to the areas where he had fought in WWII and particularly to the area where he had been wounded in action. Later, she would laugh and say she had made a mistake in giving us the trip because we wanted to go overseas every year.

Harold Storey:

Rena's mother's sister, Rachel Wheeler, had come to live with her, and as we traveled, they had planned to look after our children, who were thirteen and nine years old at the time. The only stipulation was that Rena and I should take separate flights and fly on separate planes. Her reasoning was that if one plane went down, odds were the other one would not, leaving one parent to raise the children! It was an idea with which I fully agreed. (I thought about that especially when Rena and I led a trip to Europe with fifteen girls of our daughter's age her junior year in high school. What were we thinking?) At the time, Rena was teaching an art enrichment program at Thornwood School for girls in Rome.

In April 1966 we took our first trip, booked on two separate flights, and were to arrive and meet at Orly airport near Paris. This plan fell apart right away when my plane was delayed for hours and my arrival was later than Rena's.

Rena Storey:

My flight was diverted to Le Bourget because jet aircraft were not to land at Orly after midnight. The Le Bourget airport was a distance from Paris. It was known as Charles Lindbergh's landing place at the completion of his famous flight across the Atlantic.

When we landed, although it was a late hour, I managed to take a bus to the Paris Central Station. I found a taxi to take me to the Hotel Ambassador, although I had nothing to show for a reservation. Nevertheless, I arrived a bit rattled, and the clerk recognized I was distressed.

By then it was 3:00 AM. He assured me they had notice of our arrival. When Harold did arrive at 7:00 AM, the same clerk called to say, "Mr. Storey is here. I am so glad for you!" He wasn't half as glad as I was after my first flight overseas. We decided we would travel together as soon as the children grew up.

Harold Storey:

After our eventful arrival, we drove to the Alsace-Lorraine region, to the site of the momentous Moselle River crossing. In September 1944 the platoon I had led across that cold and dangerous river is where our accomplishment earned for me the Silver Star.

From there we drove to the city of Metz, France, which was defeated after the Moselle crossing, and then on to Luxembourg, where I was wounded in combat outside the village of Diekirch. Afterward, I had been taken to a church in Diekirch that was being used as a first-aid station. When I walked into that church, my memories of the war came flooding back.

Rena Storey:

This trip became unforgettable to me in two ways. First, I was able to see the areas that Harold had described so many times, making it possible for me to be able to connect the events that took place in the areas. Second, as we traveled, I had the opportunity to fulfill a wish of mine to see many of the works of art I had studied in college.

Harold Storey:

It was indeed unforgettable. More than we would ever imagine, this trip was to shape our future years in memories and in our love for sharing many valuable travels.

Rena Storey:

Harold is a social being who is sensitive, resourceful, gregarious, of strong opinion, fearless at times, and able to debate anyone (a former member of the University of Georgia's Demosthenian Literary Society). Above all, Harold wants to change the world for the better.

His exploration of so many subjects, current and past, keeps him interested and interesting.

Living for months in combat as a foot soldier in Europe during World War II was a defining and transforming experience in Harold's life. With death occurring all around him, life took on a very different meaning.

Harold's parents were also a big influence in the formation of his character. Their faith and example of helping others led him to form his own faith as a Christian. His strong bonds with his parents spilled over into the bonds between us as husband and wife, and between us and our children and grandchildren.

Faith is very much a part of who Harold is. When we were dating, his values and morality all resonated with me. His love for his family and compassion for others were a part of my upbringing as well, taught by my parents' example.

Harold Storey:

Similar beliefs are important in any marriage. Often they are the glue that holds relationships together. When our ups and downs have occurred, as they do in any healthy, growing relationship, Rena and I have been able to forgive and move on, and to love and accept each other.

Our regular evening family talk times and late-night visits with friends and neighbors are a big part of our lives. The laughter we share openly over stories of those ups and downs, differences and how we resolved them, and how they played out have given us ample time to laugh at ourselves and appreciate each other more deeply.

Rena Storey:

My husband is generous to a fault, and he is a risk-taker when it comes to helping people. You could call him a "soft touch." He usually errs on the side of generosity at first, and sometimes that generosity is misused, but he usually realizes that and reacts as he sees fit.

He also has been encouraging to me. More than once I have been able to move out of my comfort zone with his support. Both of us think truth told in humor is easier to swallow. A sense of humor along with wit is one of Harold's trademarks. When Harold once asked a fairly new employee to look for a missing object, the employee replied, "That's not in my domain." Harold's quick reply was, "It is now!"

Harold and Rena:

We have been "in each other's domain" for seventy years. We hope our lives have had a positive impact on those whom we have met and with whom we have worked over all these years. Our life together has for both of us been meaningful and fulfilling. We are both very grateful.

Rena Mebane Storey and I. Harold Storey

CPSIA information can be obtained
at www.ICGtesting.com
Printed in the USA
BVHW041427091221
623633BV00011B/727

9 781635 281224